Aspen & Central Colorado

TRAILS

A Hiking Guide

Warren Ohlrich
2nd Edition

WHO PRESS • BASALT, COLORADO

PUBLISHED BY

WHO Press
0311 West Sopris Creek Road
Basalt, CO 81621

Library of Congress Catalog Card Number: 99-71140

ISBN 1-882426-12-6

Printed in the United States of America

All photos by Karen B. Ohlrich
except for the following by Warren H. Ohlrich:
pp. 41, 43, 57, 58

Cover photo by Karen B. Ohlrich

Cover design and maps by Curt Carpenter

Table of Contents

Introduction

Hiking is the single most important outdoor activity in the Aspen and Central Colorado area during the summer. *Aspen-Snowmass Trails* is the basic manual for hikers in the Aspen/Snowmass area. However, for those who have hiked most of the trails listed in that guide, or are looking for more isolated and less well-known trails, *Aspen and Central Colorado Trails* covers a variety of routes not included in *Aspen-Snowmass Trails*. This guide also covers a broader area, including the Fryingpan and Crystal River valleys, Leadville, and the area between Aspen and Crested Butte.

The trails in this book are almost all are in designated Wilderness areas. While the majority of the routes are day hikes, many can be extended into overnight trips. All 36 routes, with the exception of Route #20, are maintained by the Forest Service, making route-finding relatively easy. However, many of the trails lead to areas above timberline where exploration without the benefit of maintained trails can add another dimension to the hikes.

Many of the routes also include a scenic drive to the trailhead. All of the hikes in the Fryingpan River Valley involve at least a 30-mile drive up this beautiful valley on a winding road alongside the Fryingpan River and Ruedi Reservoir. The hikes off Lincoln Creek Road, Hagerman Pass Road, and Capitol Creek Road involve driving somewhat isolated and rough stretches of gravel road to reach the trailhead. It's always best to plan an entire day for these routes to enjoy them to the fullest.

Various aids can be very helpful on your trip. The USGS 7.5-minute topography maps and the *Trails Illustrated* maps are listed for each route. The routes in this guide are described well enough so that separate maps are not absolutely necessary, but maps give a good perspective of what lies around you. A map can also be invaluable when, for whatever reason, you stray from the trail. A compass and altimeter also make route-finding easier. The elevation for each trailhead is listed accurately and can be used to set an altimeter. The elevation range translates somewhat into the difficulty of the hike. Be aware that the portions of trails at higher elevations are often snow-covered early in the summer, with some of the higher passes not losing their snow cover until well into July.

Since most of the trails are in Wilderness areas, a section entitled "Wilderness" has been included for a better understanding of how hikers should conduct themselves in the Wilderness. It is also wise to familiarize yourself with all the current regulations for the backcountry by visiting the local Forest Service Office and by reading the signs at the trailheads.

The information board and trail register which is found at most trailheads.

A number of precautions should be taken on any of these hikes. Take the high altitude in this area into account—if not acclimated, your trip will take longer, and dizziness, headaches, lack of appetite, and nausea can be signs of altitude sickness. It's almost imperative to start your hikes early in the day; sudden thunderstorms in the afternoons are very common in these mountains, even if the sky is clear earlier. For this reason it's also necessary to carry rain gear and extra clothing on all but the very shortest hikes. Lightning and thunderstorms are especially severe and dangerous above treeline (usually about 11,500 feet). Sunglasses and sun screen are also imperative on all hikes in the high country because of the intense sun at higher elevations.

You should also carry an adequate supply of water (about 1 pint per person for 3 miles)—you can no longer drink out of any water sources in the backcountry without filtering or treating the water; giardia is prevalent at all altitudes. Giardia is a microscopic organism found in water which can cause fever, nausea, weakness, and diarrhea. Giardia can also be destroyed by boiling the water for 5 minutes.

Stay dry and warm while hiking. Hypothermia is a lowering of the body's core temperature which can lead to death. Symptoms include shivering, tiredness, slurred speech, and disorientation. Anyone suffering from hypothermia should be kept warm and dry, and given hot drinks, but no alcohol. Immediate professional medical assistance will be necessary.

Wilderness

Since the late 1800s selected public lands have been protected from uncontrolled development and reserved to benefit the Nation as a whole. This process was formalized in the Wilderness Act of 1964. Objectives for preserving the Wilderness system include: perpetuating a long-lasting system of high quality Wilderness that represents natural ecosystems; providing opportunities for public use and enjoyment of the Wilderness resource; allowing plants and animals indigenous to the area to develop through natural processes; maintaining watersheds and airsheds in a healthy condition; protecting threatened or endangered plant and animal species. User comfort is not an objective—Wilderness exists for its own intrinsic values.

Trails in the following six Wilderness areas are included in this hiking trail guide: Maroon Bells-Snowmass Wilderness, Collegiate Peaks Wilderness, Hunter Fryingpan Wilderness, Mount Massive Wilderness, Holy Cross Wilderness, and the Raggeds Wilderness.

Wilderness Ethics

LESSEN YOUR IMPACT

Limit the size of your group. Groups under 10 people have less impact on the Wilderness

Shortcuts cause erosion. Please stay on the established trail which is designed to minimize erosion, protect vegetation, and maintain a comfortable grade.

Leave rocks, flowers, wood, antlers, and other interesting items in their natural state for others to enjoy. Picking wildflowers is punishable by law. "Take only memories, leave only footprints."

Do not feed wildlife. Your food or leftovers can upset the natural balance of their food chain or cause bacteria harmful to them.

Watch your step—the alpine tundra is delicate. Above timberline, walk on trails, rocks, or snow when possible.

Leave mechanization behind. Use of motorized/mechanical transport and equipment (including mountain bikes) within the Wilderness is prohibited.

ANIMALS IN THE BACKCOUNTRY

Keep dogs on a leash at all times. Loose dogs can harass wildlife and create conflicts between visitors. Pets are not a natural part of the Wilderness; their presence can disrupt wildlife. You are encouraged to leave your dogs or other pets at home.

Do not hobble, picket or tether horses within 100 feet of lakes, streams and trails. This helps keep lakes and streams clean and pure.

CAMPING

Camp only on hard ground at least 100 feet away from streams, lakes and trails. This will reduce your impact on the environment and increase your privacy. Vegetation and soils adjacent to lakes and streams are extremely sensitive to disturbance. Respect "No Camping Here" or "Closed for Revegetation" signs and choose another campsite.

Use a lightweight backpacking stove instead of building a campfire. Campfires leave a permanent scar on rocks and soil. Gas stoves don't deplete your Wilderness wood-fuel resources, especially in the high country above 10,000 feet where wood is being burned faster than it's produced.

Wash at least 100 feet away from water source and throw out dirty water away from water source. Use biodegradable soap. Don't wash or bathe in the lake or stream; even biodegradable soap pollutes if it goes directly into the water.

Keep your noise level low. Unnecessary loud noise may frighten wildlife and annoy other Wilderness visitors.

Pack out what you pack in. Please pick up anyone else's trash you may find along the way. Leave your campsite in a natural state. Remember, aluminum and plastic don't burn!

SANITATION

Bury feces. Use a small trowel to bury human waste at least 6 inches deep and at least 100 feet away from water sources and trails. Burn or bury toilet paper. Use white toilet paper—dyes in toilet paper may be harmful to the environment.

Trail Selection Guide

#	Trail	Length	Elevation	Access
16	Braille Trail	¼ mi.	10,400	Aspen/I. Pass
1	Maroon Creek Trail	2–7 mi.	8,670–9,880	Aspen
17	Anderson/Petrol. Lakes	4 mi.	11,200–12,300	Aspen/I. Pass
19	Continental Divide	4 mi.	12,095–13,045	Ind. Pass
20	Blue Lake	4 mi.	10,880–12,495	Ind. Pass
21	Timberline Lake	4 mi.	10,020–10,855	Leadville
27	Savage Lakes	4 mi.	9,880–11,150	Fryingpan
33	Avalanche Creek Trail	5–11 mi.	7,310–8,480	Redstone
10	Hardscr./Williams Lakes	6 mi.	9,460–10,815	Snowmass
11	Thomas Lakes	6 mi.	8,640–10,260	Basalt/Carb.
2	East Maroon Trail	6–10 mi.	8,680–9,880	Aspen
6	East Snowmass Trail	6–10 mi.	8,370–11,200	Snowmass V.
22	Native Lake	7 mi.	10,800–11,860	Leadville
30	Lyle & Mormon Lakes	7 mi.	10,720–11,680	Fryingpan
5	Government Trail	8 mi.	7,900–9,460	Aspen/Snow.
18	Tabor Creek Trail	8 mi.	10,230–12,460	Aspen/I. Pass
29	Sawyer Lake	8 mi.	9,460–11,220	Fryingpan
28	Josephine Lake	9 mi.	9,240–11,560	Fryingpan
31	Fryingpan Lakes	9 mi.	9,950–11,020	Fryingpan
35	Marble Peak/Rasp. Crk.	9 mi.	7,920–11,314	Marble
3	Buckskin Pass	9.5 mi.	9,580–12,462	Aspen
7	Sunnyside/Hunter Valley	10 mi.	7,830–10,070	Aspen

25	No. Mount Elbert Trail	10 mi.	10,070–14,433	Leadville
13	W. Maroon Pass/Schofield	11 mi.	9,580–12,500	Aspen
23	Willis Lake	11 mi.	9,350–11,810	Twin Lakes
24	So. Mount Elbert Trail	11 mi.	9,550–14,433	Twin Lakes
26	Black Cloud Trail	11 mi.	9,700–14,433	Twin Lakes
8	Spruce Crk./Mt. Yeckel	12 mi.	8,690–11,765	Lenado
12	Mount Sopris	12 mi.	8,640–12,953	Basalt/Carb.
32	Granite Lakes	12 mi.	8,762–11,620	Fryingpan
36	Carbonate/Buckskin Basin	12 mi.	7,950–12,100	Marble
4	West Maroon Pass	14 mi.	9,580–12,500	Aspen
14	E. Maroon Pass/Gothic	16 mi.	8,680–11,820	Aspen
9	Woody Crk./Hunter Val.	17 mi.	8,480–11,650	Lenado
34	Avalanche/East Creek	17–25 mi.	7,150–12,120	Redstone
15	Triangle Pass/Gothic	19 mi.	8,760–12,900	Aspen

Short & easy: 1, 2, 16, 21, 33

Longer & easy: 2, 5, 22, 29, 31, 33

Beautiful/adventurous drive to trailhead: 8, 9, 10, 17, 18, 22, 27, 30, 31

Backpacking: 4, 8, 9, 13, 14, 15, 22, 23, 27, 28, 30, 31, 32, 34, 36

Additional exploration from destination: 17, 22, 23, 27, 28, 30, 31, 32, 34

Cascading streams: 18, 20, 27, 29, 32, 33, 34, 36

Aspen/Snowmass

Aspen, once a booming mining town, is now famous for downhill skiing and cultural events such as the Aspen Music Festival. The summer visitors to Aspen have also discovered that the Aspen/Snowmass area offers some of the best Wilderness hiking in the Continental United States. The 12 routes below represent some of the hiking available in the Roaring Fork Valley, which is flanked by the Maroon Bells-Snowmass Wilderness and the Hunter Fryingpan Wilderness. Of the hikes close to Aspen and Snowmass Village, Routes #1–4, the hikes in the vicinity of the Maroon Bells (two 14,000-foot peaks at the end of the Maroon Valley), are the most popular. Routes #5-7, mostly wooded trails, are also easily accessible from Aspen and Snowmass Village. For longer more solitary hikes, try Routes #8 & #9 from the ghost town of Lenado in the Woody Creek Valley. Route #10 is a peaceful, wooded hike to two lakes. Route #11 takes you to two scenic lakes at the foot of Mount Sopris, and #12 is the continuation up to the summit of this prominent Roaring Fork Valley peak.

1. Maroon Creek Trail

Start/Destination: Maroon Lake (9,580 feet)
Round-trip Distance/Hiking Time: 2–7 miles/1–4 hours
Elevation Range: 8,670–9,800 feet
Maps: p. 12; USGS Maroon Bells, Highland Peak; TI # 128
Wilderness Designation: Non-Wilderness

General Comments: The Maroon Creek Trail offers the opportunity to get a good, close look at some of the notable features of the Maroon Valley, such as the many avalanche paths, beaver ponds, wildflowers, aspen, and the tall bordering peaks. You can follow the trail downhill along the creek from Maroon Lake for a short distance and retrace your steps, or you can continue down to the East Maroon Trailhead at the East Maroon Portal (3.5 miles). A shorter option is to make a 2-mile loop of the two branches of the Maroon Creek Trail from Maroon Lake.

Directions to Trailhead: To reach Maroon Lake from Highway 82, turn south onto Maroon Creek Road one-half mile west of Aspen and continue up Maroon Creek Road 9.5 miles to the day parking lot near Maroon Lake. During the summer the road beyond the T Lazy 7 Ranch is closed to automobile traffic from about 8:30 A.M.–5:00 P.M.; during this time it is necessary to take a bus from Aspen to get to Maroon Lake.

Trail Route: (1) Maroon Creek Trail to East Maroon Portal: Follow the Maroon Creek Trail #1982 toward the outlet stream at the north end of Maroon Lake and cross the bridge over Maroon Creek. Go left on the trail which follows the right side of the rushing creek down the valley. Above the trail is an avalanche slide area, upvalley are the Maroon Bells, and ahead are vistas of the Maroon Valley. In less than a mile, as you enter some trees, you will come to a bridge across the creek on your left. To continue down to the East Maroon Portal, stay straight along the right side of West Maroon Creek until at about 2 miles below Maroon Lake you come to a little knoll (good picnic spot) right above the confluence of the East and West Maroon creeks. Just beyond the knoll cross the bridge and stay left as the trail gradually ascends to a junction with the East Maroon Trail. Continue left here and head down the valley. In about 30–40 minutes you will come to a bridge on the left crossing over into the East Maroon Portal parking lot. From the parking lot you can walk up to the road to catch a ride up to Maroon Lake, or you can retrace your route on the trail.

(2) Maroon Creek Trail Loop: For this shorter 2-mile loop from Maroon Lake, take the west branch of the Maroon Creek Trail from Maroon Lake north toward West Maroon Portal. In 20–30 minutes at West Maroon Portal cross the road and pick up the trail on the other side as it passes through a meadow with good views of the Bells and Maroon Valley. Just beyond the open area the trail crosses a bridge over the beautiful, rushing West Maroon Creek. Go left about 30 feet and then follow the trail up to the right as it heads up the valley, crossing below avalanche chutes and through rockslides, with scenic vistas in every direction. In less than a mile you will cross a bridge and come to the start of the loop at Maroon Lake.

2. East Maroon Trail

Start/Destination: East Maroon Trailhead (8,680 feet)
Round-trip Distance/Hiking Time: 6–10 miles/4–7 hours
Elevation Range: 8,680–9,880 feet
Maps: p. 12; USGS Maroon Bells, Highland Peak; TI #128
Wilderness Designation: Maroon Bells-Snowmass Wilderness

General Comments: The East Maroon Trail ascends very gradually up the East Maroon Valley and is an excellent route for anyone looking for an easy, pleasant, day hike of up to 10 miles without encountering the crowds generally found at Maroon Lake. The hike starts in the Maroon Valley and continues along East Maroon Creek below the eastern slopes of 14,018-foot Pyramid Peak. The most prominent features of the valley are the many avalanche paths coming down the valley walls. In September the East

The magnificent Maroon Bells.

Maroon Valley is ablaze with the golden color of the aspen. The turnaround point for anyone wishing to do a round trip of 10 miles is the first stream crossing, which is usually impassable earlier in the summer. Hikers should give the right of way to any horseback riders that they encounter on the trail.

Directions to Trailhead: From Highway 82 one-half mile west of Aspen turn south onto Maroon Creek Road. Drive 6.3 miles up Maroon Creek Road and turn left down a road leading to the parking lot at East Maroon Portal. During the summer the Maroon Creek Road is generally closed to auto traffic from about 8:30 A.M. to 5:00 P.M. Check the latest bus regulations for drop-off and pickup at the East Maroon Trailhead, or get an early start.

Trail Route: From the parking lot go across the bridge and follow the trail to the right. Maroon Creek will be on the right as you pass through meadows and beautiful stands of aspen. Pyramid Peak looms ahead and the Maroon Bells can be seen at times up the valley to the right.

In a little over a mile the Maroon Creek Trail forks off to the right; keep going straight on the East Maroon Trail and you will pass a sign indicating the Wilderness boundary. The trail climbs steadily above a small canyon created by East Maroon Creek; as you get beyond the canyon watch for beaver ponds down by the creek. The valley soon opens up with meadows and wildflowers becoming more frequent.

At about 4 miles stay straight as a trail branches off to the right and leads to a horse camp down by the river. After another one-half mile the trail passes by the ruins of two old cabins—this is an ideal spot for a picnic. Just after crossing a large avalanche area the trail makes a short final descent to the stream crossing which marks the turnaround point. Follow the same route back, with the option of descending to the Maroon Creek Trail on the way and following it up to Maroon Lake.

3. Buckskin Pass

Start/Destination: Maroon Lake/Buckskin Pass (9,580/12,462 feet)
Round-trip Distance/Hiking Time: 9.5 miles/7 hours
Elevation Range: 9580–12,462 feet
Maps: p. 12; USGS Maroon Bells; TI #128
Wilderness Designation: Maroon Bells-Snowmass Wilderness

General Comments: The trip to Buckskin Pass on this beautiful, very popular, well-worn route is generally accomplished as a day hike by the acclimated and fit, and involves an elevation gain of almost 3,000 feet. The camping is good in the scenic, treed Minnehaha Gulch for those who wish to extend the trip over two or three days. It is almost imperative to start early as thunderstorms are fairly common on the pass in the early afternoon. The first part of the hike is highlighted by views of Maroon Lake, Crater Lake, the Maroon Bells, and Pyramid Peak. The upper part of the hike goes through a beautiful basin surrounded by peaks and full of wildflowers. From the pass a panorama of Snowmass Lake, 14,092-foot Snowmass Mountain, 14,130-foot Capitol Peak, Mount Daly, and other prominent peaks unfolds to the west.

Directions to Trailhead: (Same as Route #1, Maroon Creek Trail)

Trail Route: From Maroon Lake watch for the sign indicating the Maroon-Snowmass Trail, which goes up along the west side of Maroon Lake; you will be following the Maroon-Snowmass Trail all the way to Buckskin Pass. After passing through the field of wildflowers above Maroon Lake, stay right at the trail intersection at the end of the lake. This rocky, rough trail ascends through the aspen past several intersections to the left which head down to the beaver ponds and the Scenic Trail. Continue to stay right and you will be ascending through a treed and rocky area with the Maroon Bells towering ahead as you break out into the open.

From the top of Minnehaha Gulch, Buckskin Pass is visible in the distance.

After a short, gradual descent through a rocky area toward Crater Lake you will come to a trail junction in the aspen about 1¾ miles from the start of your hike. Take the Maroon-Snowmass Trail to the right toward Buckskin Pass and Snowmass Lake. From here you will climb steadily through the trees and enter Minnehaha Gulch in about a mile with the steep slopes of the Maroon Bells rising up on the other side of the gulch. After about one-half mile you will make an easy stream crossing and in another one-half mile will exit the gulch into a big, open expanse with Buckskin Pass visible ahead.

Your climb continues through rocks, scrub growth, meadows, and past a couple of cascading streams. About 15–20 minutes from the top of Minnehaha Gulch you will come to a well-signed fork in the trail. The Willow Lake Trail goes right and the Maroon-Snowmass Trail continues straight ahead. Stay straight for a steady climb through alpine meadows full of wildflowers.

The last section of trail up to the rocky pass switchbacks somewhat steeply through some rocks and slopes which are bespeckled by a variety of different colored wildflowers. When you finally reach the pass, the vistas in every direction make the trip very worthwhile. For the trip back down follow the same route.

4. West Maroon Pass

Start/Destination: Maroon Lake/West Maroon Pass (9,580/12,500 feet)
Round-trip Distance/Hiking Time: 14 miles/2 days
Elevation Range: 9,580–12,500 feet
Maps: p. 12; USGS Maroon Bells; TI #128
Wilderness Designation: Maroon Bells-Snowmass Wilderness

General Comments: The trail to West Maroon Pass follows a classic valley route and offers great wildflower viewing and a chance to see the Elk Mountain Range from a spectacular 12,500-foot mountain pass. Only the very athletic and fit go all the way to the pass on a day hike (with a very early start). However, a hike part way up the trail is an excellent day trip. This trail can also be used for a day trip to Crested Butte (see Route #13). For those taking the two-day round trip to the pass, the good camping spots are in the last groups of trees before the pass. Many backpackers use this route as part of a multi-day trip around the Maroon Bells (see *Aspen-Snowmass Trails*, Route #29). Early in the summer when the water is high the two stream crossings may be impassible, or treacherous to cross, so be prepared.

Directions to Trailhead: (Same as Route #1, Maroon Creek Trail)

Trail Route: From Maroon Lake watch for the sign indicating the Maroon-Snowmass Trail, which goes up along the west side of Maroon Lake. Stay right at the trail intersection at the end of Maroon Lake. This rocky, rough trail ascends through aspen and spruce past several intersections on the left which head down to the beaver ponds and the Scenic Trail. Continue to stay right on a steady uphill.

As the trail reaches the top of a rocky rise and breaks into the open, the prominent Maroon Bells dominate the landscape directly ahead. After a short, gradual descent through a rocky area toward Crater Lake you will come to a trail junction in the aspen about 1¾ miles from the start of your hike. Take the West Maroon Trail #1970 left and stay along the right side of Crater Lake on the main, well-worn trail which heads toward the West Maroon Valley. For a few hundred yards beyond the lake the trail will follow the creek closely and then head up through the trees before climbing into the open valley through a rock field covered with columbines and other wildflowers. Ahead the valley walls are rimmed by rocky peaks with an occasional waterfall tumbling down.

About 1½ miles past Crater Lake you will come to the first stream crossing where there's a good chance of getting your feet wet trying to cross. Make sure to go straight across at this point to pick up the trail directly on the other side as it goes up onto a little plateau. After a pretty 25-minute walk through patches of woods, scrub willows, and wildflowers you will have to cross the creek again just as the trail breaks out into the open. Between these two stream crossings are many good places to camp, but a few more lie ahead.

The valley now spreads out before you as you continue on a steady climb for about 15 minutes to the last group of trees that would provide shelter for camping. From here the trail heads up somewhat steeply into the tundra through numerous patches of wildflowers. After gaining some more altitude, you will soon be able to see the trail in the distance angling steeply up toward the pass on the rocky ridge to the right. After a couple of switchbacks and a long climbing traverse to the top, you will reach West Maroon Pass, engulfed in a world of rock and ridges. The trail continuing on the other side of the pass follows the East Fork to the Schofield Pass Road which leads to Gothic and Crested Butte (see Route #13). Hopefully, you brought a camera to record this occasion.

One of the views from West Maroon Pass.

5. Government Trail

Start/Destination: Snowmass Village/Aspen (9,080/8,030 feet)
One-way Distance/Hiking Time: 8 miles/5–6 hours
Elevation Range: 7,900–9,460 feet
Maps: p. 20; USGS Highland Peak, Aspen; TI #127, 128
Wilderness Designation: Non-Wilderness

General Comments: This hike between Aspen and Snowmass Village is popular with hikers, bikers, and, in the winter, cross-country skiers. The Government Trail (also known as the Brush Creek Trail) offers hiking opportunities in the spring and fall when most other mountain trails are covered with snow. The trail is beautifully wooded with aspen and pine; a number of mountain streams cross the trail, adding to its picturesque quality, but sometimes creating muddy spots. The trail crosses the Buttermilk ski slopes which are full of wildflowers in the spring and summer. In September, when the aspen are turning color, the Government Trail becomes a carpet of gold.

Since the trailheads are so accessible to Aspen and Snowmass Village, most hikers do this as a one-way trip and get a ride back. The easier direction to hike is from Snowmass Village to Aspen, which involves a loss of elevation. However, since it can easily be hiked in either direction, both routes are described below. Due to the trail's popularity with mountain bikers, it's best to start your hike early in the morning when less bikers normally would be encountered. Please do not stray from the trail, since much of it is on privately owned property, and trespassing could endanger the future of the trail's use.

Directions to Trailheads: (1) To get to the Snowmass Village trailhead, turn south onto Brush Creek Road from Highway 82 six miles west of Aspen. Go 4.7 miles to Wood Road and turn left. Follow Wood Road uphill for 2.2 miles to Pine Lane (marked private). Go up Pine Lane about 150 yards to the gravel road on the left for the mountain access parking. Go about 300 yards up the road to the parking lot at the trailhead.

(2) For the Aspen trailhead turn south onto Maroon Creek Road from Highway 82 one-half mile west of Aspen. Go just over one mile to Iselin Park on the right and park. The trailhead is at the south end of the tennis courts. *(Note: This trailhead may change when a new bridge is constructed over Maroon Creek.)*

Trail Route: (1) Snowmass Village trailhead: From the parking lot go down the ski access road which then gradually ascends across several ski slopes and under a couple of lifts. At the fork in the road stay straight

toward Elk Camp. Just after passing below the Elk Camp Lift, you will come to aspen trees at the edge of the ski area. From here the Government Trail goes left into the trees and descends, crosses another trail, crosses East Brush Creek and a couple of smaller streams, and continues to delightfully meander up and down through the woods.

At about two miles the trail passes through a large clearing and crosses a stream, then heads up along the left side of the stream before leveling off through a peaceful pine forest and descending through the aspen. At about 4 miles stay straight on the trail toward Buttermilk as you cross Owl Creek and walk along a fence on your left above Whites Lake. In another one-half mile the trail goes straight as a faded jeep trail forks down to the left. A sign here should indicate that you're on the Brush Creek Trail.

After crossing a rocky section on a steep slope in the aspen, the trail comes out onto the West Buttermilk ski slopes. Do not cut down the slopes, but stay on the trail as it crosses the slopes and descends through the woods. After a few switchbacks through the trees the trail traverses a Main Buttermilk ski slope, follows some steep switchbacks down the side of a hill, and heads on toward the Tiehack Ski Area. Pay attention to any trail signs; the routing through this area could change from time to time due to private property. As you leave the Tiehack Ski Area beyond Lift #5, you can see Iselin Park ahead with the ball diamond, the school area, and all of Aspen spread out in the distance. From here the trail winds down, quite steeply in places, to Maroon Creek, where you cross on a bridge and take a steep climb up the other side of the creek to the trailhead at Iselin Park on Maroon Creek Road.

(2) Aspen trailhead at Iselin Park: Follow the path around the south side of the tennis courts and walk down the steep side of the gully to the bridge over the creek. Just beyond the bridge on the left the trail heads steeply up the embankment. After steep switchbacks the trail crosses the upper slopes of Tiehack Ski Area, climbs uphill through aspen, crosses Main Buttermilk ski slopes, and climbs uphill some more to the West Buttermilk ski slopes.

At the 3-mile point the trail leaves the ski slopes and goes through a rocky section in the aspen. Continue to go straight along the left side of a fenced-off area as you stay above Whites Lake. You will be going through lovely stands of aspen and pine, and may encounter deer in here. At about five miles the trail starts dropping along the right side of a stream, then crosses it and soon heads through a clearing. At the end of the clearing a sign indicates that the Government Trail goes up to the left as another trail branches off to the right. From the aspen ahead you will get some good views of the Snowmass Club golf course and the Brush Creek Valley. After traversing the side of a gully you will start a series of stream crossings.

After the East Brush Creek crossing the trail climbs steeply through the aspen to the Snowmass Ski Area and the marked beginning of the Government Trail. From here follow the ski service road downhill, under a lift, and down No Name ski trail. Keep following the road down as it passes under two more lifts, then above the Wood Run lift to the parking lot.

6. East Snowmass Trail

Start/Destination: East Snowmass Trailhead (8,370 feet)
Round-trip Distance/Hiking Time: 6–10 miles/4–7 hours
Elevation Range: 8,370–10,100/11,200 feet
Maps: p. 20; USGS Highland Peak; TI #128
Wilderness Designation: Maroon Bells-Snowmass Wilderness

General Comments: The East Snowmass Trail is located in a beautiful valley just to the west of the Snowmass Ski Area and is usually overlooked by most hikers. The trail is steep in places and covers varying terrain along East Snowmass Creek. It passes through groves of conifers with good camping and picnic sites, and through alpine meadows with views of jagged granite formations, waterfalls, red rock cliffs, and high rugged mountains. As described here this trail is a pleasant day hike—you can end your hike anywhere and return down the trail to the trailhead. However, it is also possible to make this into a 2–3 day trip by continuing up to the 12,690-foot pass at the end of the valley and on to Willow Lake beyond the pass (see Route #23 in *Aspen-Snowmass Trails*).

Directions to Trailhead: (1) From Highway 82:Drive to Old Snowmass turnoff (14 miles northwest of Aspen, 3.6 miles southeast of Basalt bypass light) and turn south at the gas station. Go 1.8 miles to Snowmass Creek Road and turn left. Go 9.1 miles to a bridge and one-quarter mile past the bridge turn right at the "T". The trailhead is on the left in the trees, 250–300 yards from the turn.

(2) From Snowmass Village: Turn onto Divide Road from Brush Creek Road (5.3 miles from Highway 82, just below the Snowmass Village Mall). At just under a mile you will pass Krabloonik and continue down a somewhat rough gravel, rocky road through the Campground section of the Snowmass Ski Area. After 1.6 miles from Krabloonik at a fork stay straight and look for the trailhead on the left in the woods in 250–300 yards. If you reach the end of the road and a parking area for the trailhead for the Maroon-Snowmass Trail, then you've gone one-quarter mile too far.

Trail Route: The trail starts out ascending fairly steeply, first through aspen, then spruce and pine, as it initially heads away from the creek. After about two-thirds of a mile the trail levels off somewhat and soon continues on a gradual climb above East Snowmass Creek with the steep, rocky valley wall off to the left. Just over one mile from the start, in a small grassy open area, follow a fork in the trail to the right where a sign indicates the East Snowmass Trail #1977. The trail continues climbing through trees and occasional small open areas abounding with wildflowers as you catch views of the rocky valley walls and avalanche paths off to the sides. After climbing high above the roaring stream, the trail levels off a little, before climbing out into the open at just over two miles from the trailhead.

The trail continues through the middle of the valley through scrub willow, fields of wildflowers, and occasional clumps of spruce trees. After another 1½ miles you will pass through a pleasant conifer forest before again breaking out into the open with a knoll ahead and the end of the valley in sight. You can see the pass in the distance and the rocky ridges and cliffs in all directions. The meadow here is a good place to picnic and turn around, or you can continue farther to explore the tundra and wildflowers ahead.

7. Sunnyside/Hunter Valley Loop

Start/Destination: Sunnyside Trailhead/Hunter Valley Trailhead by Hunter Creek Condominiums (7,830/7,850 feet)
Round-trip Distance/Hiking Time: 10 miles/6–7 hours
Elevation Range: 7,830–10,070 feet
Maps: p. 24; USGS Aspen; TI #127
Wilderness Designation: Non-Wilderness

General Comments: This route follows the Sunnyside Trail high along Red Mountain on the north side of Aspen and drops into beautiful alpine meadows in Hunter Valley on the Hunter Valley Trail. The easy accessibility of this route and the views of Aspen, the Roaring Fork Valley, and the Elk Mountain Range make this a very enjoyable local hike. The trail passes through some of the most beautiful stands of aspen trees in the Aspen area. Grouse, deer, fox, and other wildlife are frequently seen on this route. Be sure to follow the trail directions carefully—it's easy to get lost.

Directions to Trailhead: Take the Snowbunny Bus to Red Butte Drive (last stop on Cemetery Lane) and walk another .4 miles north (uphill) on McLain Flats Road (continuation of Cemetery Lane) to the trailhead on the right. If driving, go west on Highway 82 from Aspen to Cemetery Lane just before the golf course and go right on Cemetery Lane for 1.5 miles (one-third mile past the bridge over Roaring Fork River) to a small parking area on left. The trailhead is just across the road.

This trailhead can also be reached on foot from the center of Aspen by taking the 1¾-mile Rio Grande paved trail to McLain Flats Road (see *Aspen-Snowmass Trails* Route #7) and then going right one-third mile.

Trail Route: The Sunnyside Trail climbs steeply through sagebrush, scrub oak, and wildflowers on Red Mountain. At 1 mile the trail crosses an irrigation ditch and the driveway of a mountain home. From this point it climbs another two-thirds of a mile before entering the aspen trees. In the trees you will pass some antennas as the trail levels a little before climbing steeply again through the aspen. You will soon find yourself on a ridge following a fairly level trail (with one climb thrown in) through beautiful uniform stands of aspen.

Soon after the spot you leveled off on top you will come to a trail junction, the intersection of Sunnyside and the Shadyside Trail (may or may not be marked by a sign). Stay right on the Sunnyside Trail along the south side of the mountain. Again you will have good views of Aspen to the right as the trail gradually descends through spruce and aspen. A little over a mile past the fork the remains of two old cabins can be seen on the right in a grove of aspen.

About one-half mile past the old cabins you will pass to the left of a small clearing, enter a larger clearing, and go through the left side of a third clearing. The trail will then exit onto a jeep road which you will take a couple of hundred yards to the intersection with the Shadyside Trail. Go right on the Sunnyside Trail. Follow the jeep road for about 15 minutes through a level forest of spruce, pine, and a few aspen. Just as the road starts to drop down to the left, the Sunnyside Trail leaves the road, heading down to the right through a few large pine trees. This intersection should be marked by a small sign, but it is very easy to miss unless you are paying close attention. The trail descends down a gulch through aspen trees to another jeep road, where the Sunnyside Trail ends and you pick up the Hunter Valley Trail on the other side of the road. (*Note: The crossing jeep road is the Hunter Creek Trail.*)

Continue down the Hunter Valley Trail into the valley where the trail forks in a meadow just past a small water culvert under the trail. Take the left fork to a jeep road and then left past an old cabin to Hunter Creek. Go right over the plank bridge and take an immediate right onto the trail alongside the creek. For the next 25–30 minutes you'll be passing through some of the picturesque meadows of Hunter Valley as you gradually descend along the left side of Hunter Creek.

At the National Forest boundary sign the trail enters the trees and crosses an intersecting road that leads to a private bridge on the right. Follow the trail straight ahead downstream along the creek. After about one-third mile you

One of the views of Aspen and the Aspen Mountain Ski Area from the Sunnyside Trail.

will cross the Benedict Bridge. Take an immediate left on the other side of the bridge on the footpath descending through the trees and boulders along Hunter Creek. Sometimes a little climbing over some boulders is necessary and there may be optional routes, but stay on the most worn path to the right of the creek. You will cross a second bridge, descend steeply down some steps built into the trail and fork to the right to cross another bridge at the bottom of these steps. From here you will be going through some scrub growth, then will cross an irrigation ditch, Hunter Creek, and several small streams before you reach the end of the trail at the Hunter Creek Condominiums. From here it is only one-half mile to the center of Aspen. You can go left on the road to the bus stop or right to walk into Aspen or to get to the Rio Grande Trail.

If you have to pick up a car at the Sunnyside Trailhead, take the Hunter Creek Bus to Rubey Park and the Snowbunny Bus to Red Butte Drive and walk .4 miles to the trailhead. If you take the Rio Grande Trail, it is about 2½ miles to the Sunnyside Trailhead.

8. Spruce Creek/Mount Yeckel

Start/Destination: Woody Creek Trailhead/Mount Yeckel (8,690/11,765 feet)
Round-trip Distance/Hiking Time: 12 miles/1–2 days
Elevation Range: 8,690–11,765 feet
Maps: p. 24; USGS Meredith, Aspen, Thimble Rock; TI #126, 127
Wilderness Designation: Hunter Fryingpan Wilderness

General Comments: This area has recently been added to the Hunter Fryingpan Wilderness. A hike along this very lightly traveled, wooded trail offers a variety of experiences, the highlight of which is the spectacular view of the surrounding mountains from the top of Mount Yeckel. The drive up the Woody Creek Canyon to the historic almost ghost town of Lenado, partly up a narrow gravel road, is a scenic trip itself. The hike follows two streams, Woody Creek and Spruce Creek, and passes through some peaceful conifer forests. Wildlife is plentiful and there are plenty of good places to picnic or to camp, including the partly treed summit of Mount Yeckel. I would recommend taking an overnight trip and enjoying the solitude, but a day trip to the summit is possible for strong hikers. Be aware that horseback groups occasionally use the area around Mount Yeckel.

Directions to Trailhead: Drive a little over 6 miles northwest of Aspen on Highway 82 to about one-half mile past (west of) the turnoff to Snowmass Village, and turn right onto the road (Smith Way) going to

The top of Mount Yeckel with the Elk Mountain Range in the background.

Woody Creek Canyon. After one-third mile turn left onto Upper River Road at the "T" just beyond the bridge. At 1.6 miles (200 hundred yards beyond the Woody Creek Tavern) take a hard right onto Woody Creek Road (Lenado Road) and drive 8.9 miles to the trailhead on the right, past the ghost town of Lenado and just before the bridge over Woody Creek.

Trail Route: The trail follows the right side of Woody Creek below some rocky cliffs until crossing the creek at about one-half mile. In another mile you will reach a very large rock slide area on the left, beyond which the trail crosses Spruce Creek. The stream tumbling down through the rocks here in an old growth forest creates one of the prettiest settings of the whole hike. From the creek crossing you will climb very steeply for several minutes through the conifers before coming to a trail junction. The trail going to the right up the hill is the Woody Creek Trail; you should stay straight ahead on trail #1927, the Spruce Creek Trail, which contours along the side of a narrow gully with the creek roaring below.

After a few minutes the trail crosses the creek and continues on a very gentle climb through a peaceful conifer forest. About two miles after the stream crossing you will come to a large open field of boulders; the trail winds around the right edge of the boulder field and starts ascending a little more steeply. As the trail traverses an open hillside and then an open meadow, it fades out in the grass. In the far upper left-hand corner of the meadow you will pick up the trail reentering the trees.

In less than a mile, after a steady climb through conifers, the trail enters Sawmill Park, a large open area. The trail you pass angling back to your left goes to Margy's Hut, a Tenth Mountain cross-country ski hut. Stay straight along the left side in the meadow (the trail has again disappeared in the grass). When you come to a corner where the trees jut out into the meadow, you will see the trail going back into the woods, about 150 yards from where you first entered the park. Before leaving Sawmill Park take time to look back at the Elk Mountain Range and the Aspen Highlands Ski Area in the distance to the south.

The trail continues up on a well-worn, wide, old jeep road. At a fork in the road stay left to take a long climbing traverse through the woods to several switchbacks up the back side of Mount Yeckel. Just before the summit will be a log cabin on the right. The summit of Yeckel is mostly meadow with a variety of wildflowers and a few trees; mountains and valleys are visible in every direction. You can see Mount Sopris, the Elk Mountain Range with Mount Daly, Snowmass Mountain, Pyramid, Capitol, and the Maroon Bells peaks, the Gore Range to the north, the Williams Mountains, and peaks on the Continental Divide and beyond. Return via the same route.

9. Woody Creek/Hunter Valley Loop

Start/Destination: Woody Creek Trailhead (8,690 feet)
Round-trip Distance/Hiking Time: 17 miles/2–3 days
Elevation Range: 8,480–11,650 feet
Maps: p. 24; USGS Aspen, Thimble Rock; TI #127
Wilderness Designation: Hunter Fryingpan Wilderness

General Comments: This mostly wooded loop below timberline close to Aspen is generally overlooked by most hikers/backpackers. Elk and deer are abundant along the entire route, and the second half of the route provides good views of the Elk Mountain Range and Hunter Valley. Camping can be done at a number of locations along the trail—the best spots are in the middle part of the hike just before and just after the high point of the hike. In a few places the trail becomes a little obscure, so follow the text description carefully. Mountain bikes may be encountered on the last section (in the non-Wilderness area) from Hunter Valley to Lenado. Be careful to respect private property in the Lenado area.

The route as described here begins and ends at Lenado. However, you could get a ride from Aspen to Lenado to start the hike, and then hike down into Aspen at the end, rather than return to Lenado (which involves elevation gain). This option makes the hike a little shorter and easier.

Directions to Trailhead: (Same as Route #8, Spruce Creek/Mt. Yeckel)

Trail Route: The trail follows the right side of Woody Creek below some rocky cliffs until it crosses the creek at about one-half mile. In another mile, just after a very large rock slide area, the trail crosses Spruce Creek. From the creek crossing the trail ascends very steeply for a few hundred yards through the conifers before coming to a trail junction. Trail #1927, the Spruce Creek Trail, goes straight and the Woody Creek Trail goes to the right up the hill. Take the right fork which leads along the left side of a valley in the trees, sometimes climbing quite steeply.

About two miles past the trail fork you will come to a stream crossing, beyond which the trail fades as you approach a large boulder field. The trail skirts along the left edge of the boulders, heads up steeply, then veers left toward another stream crossing. On the other side of the stream the trail again becomes easier to follow. After about 10–15 minutes of steep climbing, you will come out into a large, flat open area. Follow the left edge of the clearing for about 200 feet until the trail heads back into the woods on the left. After an ascent and contour through the woods, the trail comes to another clearing on the right with a creek. The trail fades here, but if you cross the field and creek you will be able to pick up the trail as it enters the woods on the other side of the clearing. In the woods the trail ascends steeply and starts curving to the right until, after about 20 minutes, it comes out on an open knoll (11,650 feet, the high point of the trip and an ideal picnic spot). Off to the left are the rugged Williams Mountains.

The trail follows the ridge a short distance before descending to the left below some rocks. This section of trail, contouring down the mountainside through scattered pines with views off to the left, is the most scenic section of trail on the trip. A steep switchbacking descent takes you to an open area, Deer Park. Stay left in the woods, and after about 1½ miles you will come out into a meadow, then into another open area with a stream in it. Stay on the main trail (watch out for a couple of false faded trails) along the left side of the stream. At the intersection of two well-worn trails stay straight along the stream on the Hunter Creek Trail. This marks the end of the Woody Creek Trail (9.7 miles from the trailhead). After 10 minutes you will cross the stream and soon will see Hunter Valley ahead of you.

About 10–15 minutes beyond the stream crossing, as you enter some aspen, you will join up with the Hunter Creek jeep trail which takes you below Bald Knob through pine and aspen for almost two miles to Van Horn Park, a large clearing. The jeep road goes straight through the park and a foot path goes off to the left. Either route can be taken, but it's best to stay left on the foot path to avoid more altitude gain. The trail contours around the south side of a mountain with Hunter Valley down below. Ahead you can see the

Maroon Bells, the ski areas, and part of Aspen. Soon the trail enters an open field where the jeep road rejoins it.

At the other end of the field in the aspen is a trail junction with signs. Here you can continue straight ahead down to Aspen, if you choose that option; otherwise head up the road to the right toward Four Corners and Lenado. After a steady climb of just under one mile you will reach Four Corners, a trail junction in a flat area at the top of your climb. Go straight toward Lenado, staying left on a foot trail after a few minutes. Soon you will start descending into the Woody Creek Valley as the trail winds and contours down the mountainside through the trees to the Woody Creek Road. Turn right and take the road .6 miles to the trailhead.

10. Hardscrabble/Williams Lakes

Start/Destination: Capitol Creek Trailhead/Williams Lake (9,460/10,815 feet)
Round-trip Distance/Hiking Time: 6 miles/4–5 hours
Elevation Range: 9,460–10,815 feet
Maps: p. 32; USGS Capitol Peak; TI #128
Wilderness Designation: Maroon Bells-Snowmass Wilderness

General Comments: This scenic route visits two wooded lakes and includes a very unique forest trail along a cascading stream on the way to Williams Lake. The main trail (Hell Roaring Trail) to the lakes follows a ridge and offers some good photo opportunities of Mount Daly and 14,130-foot Capitol Peak off to the south. Although this hike is somewhat out of the way and a little harder to get to than most, it is quite popular because of the spectacular scenery, both on the drive to the trailhead, and during the hike up the ridge to the lakes. If you have extra time, the hike up the Hell Roaring Trail to the pass beyond Williams Lake offers outstanding vistas of the Elk Mountain Range and the surrounding valleys, and has some excellent camping spots.

Directions to Trailhead: Take Highway 82 to the Old Snowmass turnoff (14 miles northwest of Aspen, 3.6 miles southeast of Basalt bypass light) and turn south at the gas station. Go 1.8 miles to the "T" and turn right onto Capitol Creek Road. The road turns to dirt after 5 miles. At 6.3 miles there is a public parking lot and at 7.2 miles is room for about 3–4 cars to park. From this point four-wheel drive or walking may be required over the last rough mile to the trailhead, although usually a two-wheel drive vehicle with a good driver can make it. At 8.2 miles from the "T" is a large parking area and the Capitol Creek Trailhead, from where you have good views of Capitol Peak and the Capitol Creek Valley to the south. If you

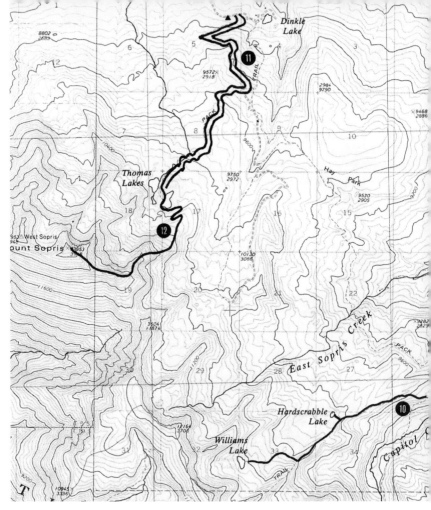

have a good four-wheel drive vehicle, you may be able to drive another mile up the very steep road (if it's open) to the Hell Roaring Trailhead.

Trail Route: From the parking lot start up the steep road into the aspen. At about two-thirds of a mile, where the road levels through the aspen, keep alert for deer and watch for a foot trail that goes straight up the ridge through a beautiful stand of aspen as the road veers off to the right. Follow this trail and in one-third mile you will come back out on the road right by the parking lot at the Hell Roaring Trailhead. Go straight ahead out of the parking lot past a green gate and along the ridge past a pond.

Following the wide trail through the conifers will take you to the intersection of the Hardscrabble Lake trail in about ten minutes. The trails here form a triangle with four large fir trees in the middle and the trail to the lake going off to the right. It's only a couple of hundred yards to the

Hardscrabble Lake, a pleasant little side trip. On getting back to the main trail, continue up the ridge through the trees, enjoy the views off to the left, and in less than a mile you will reach a little knoll, where the trail begins to drop. The trail to Williams Lake is somewhat hidden on the right about 200 feet down from the top of the knoll; many people miss this turn.

The walk to the lake is through a very pleasant conifer forest with a lot of fallen timber, boulders, ferns, and shade-loving flowers on the forest floor. The only noise is the rushing, cascading stream which you follow to the lake. In about a mile, after the last climb along the stream, you will come out onto a lake surrounded by fir trees with a red rock wall behind it. A trail goes around the lake with side trails to the many campsites. A large flat rock jutting out into the lake on your left makes an excellent picnic and fishing spot. To extend your hike, when you get back to the main trail go right up the ridge for as far as you have time. Otherwise head left down the trail back to the trailhead.

Mount Daly, Capitol Peak, and the Capitol Creek Valley as seen from the Hell Roaring Trail on the way to Williams Lake.

11. Thomas Lakes

Start/Destination: Thomas Lakes Trailhead/Thomas Lakes
(8,640/10,260 feet)
Round-trip Distance/Hiking Time: 6 miles/4 hours
Elevation Range: 8,640–10,260 feet
Maps: p. 32; USGS Mount Sopris, Basalt; TI (none)
Wilderness Designation: Maroon Bells-Snowmass Wilderness

General Comments: The two large Thomas Lakes are located in the
trees at the base of the steep face of the twin Mount Sopris peaks, a
beautiful destination for a relatively short day hike. The views of the
Roaring Fork Valley and the towering Mount Sopris are worth stopping for
along the way. The lakes have a number of designated campsites and are a
popular stopover for those hiking to the top of 12,953-foot Mount Sopris.
The Wilderness boundary is just before the lakes.

Directions to Trailhead: (1) From Aspen take Highway 82 northwest to
about 1½ miles past the Basalt bypass light and turn left onto Sopris Creek
Road. Go 1.2 miles to a "T" and turn right onto West Sopris Creek Road.
Go 5.6 miles to the top of the divide and turn left onto a dirt road, Road
311, toward Dinkle Lake. Exactly 2 miles up the road will be the parking
area on the left with the trailhead in the field on the right.

(2) From Glenwood Springs/Carbondale take Highway 133 for about 1½
miles south from Highway 82 to Prince Creek Road and turn left. Drive
about 6 miles to where Road 311 forks off to the right at the top of the
divide and follow Road 311 for 2 miles to the trailhead.

Trail Route: From the trailhead you will join up with a well-worn jeep
trail which leads to the right up through the woods. In a mile you will come
to open meadows with Mount Sopris standing out prominently ahead.
Follow the signs to Thomas Lakes and Mount Sopris as the road contours
left and then right past a side trail going toward Hay Park. The rest of the
trail to the lakes goes through aspen, then scattered trees, with meadows,
wildflowers, rocks, and views of the peak ahead.

About 10 minutes after you pass a small lake in the trees off on the right,
you will come to a fork in the trail at the Wilderness boundary sign. The
first Thomas Lake is on the right and has a very pretty aqua blue color. To
get to the second lake and the trail up Mount Sopris, take the right fork on
the main trail which stays left of the first lake as it passes a number of
campsites. In 5 minutes you will reach another trail fork with the main trail
going right. Stay left here, following the sign for Mount Sopris, and after a
couple of hundred feet you will see the second large lake off to the left.

12. Mount Sopris

Start/Destination: Thomas Lakes Trailhead/Mount Sopris
(8,640/12,953 feet)
Round-trip Distance/Hiking Time: 12 miles/8–10 hours
Elevation Range: 8,640–12,953 feet
Maps: p. 32; USGS Mount Sopris, Basalt; TI (none)
Wilderness Designation: Maroon Bells-Snowmass Wilderness

General Comments: The twin peaks of Mount Sopris dominate the
skyline of the lower Roaring Fork Valley and are a popular destination for
hikers and climbers. The route to the top is quite rugged and rocky, a very
demanding hike at high elevation that involves a lot of climbing over loose
rock. Most fit hikers do this as a day hike with a very early start from the
trailhead. However, since thunderstorms are so common here in the early
afternoon, it is preferable to hike to Thomas Lakes and camp so that the
peak can be climbed early the next morning. The route from the trailhead
gains 4,300 vertical feet; from Thomas Lakes the gain is about 2,700 feet.

The route from Thomas Lakes follows the northeast ridge up to a false
summit (12,453 feet), and then follows the main east ridge to the Sopris
summit. Figure on adding another hour to your trip if you wish to climb to
the West Sopris summit (also 12,953 feet) from the main summit. Mount
Sopris was named after Captain Richard Sopris who explored the area in
1860 and discovered Glenwood Springs.

Directions to Trailhead: (Same as Route #11, Thomas Lakes)

Trail Route: Follow the trail as described in Route #11 to the second
large Thomas Lake. The trail up Mount Sopris circles around the right side
of this last lake and starts climbing up the ridge from the lake. This section
of trail takes some long gradual, contouring switchbacks up the side of the
ridge and then follows the top of the ridge on the right side up through some
low evergreen trees and shrubs.

About one mile up from the lake the trail gets into a very rocky area where
only a few vestiges of trees and shrubs are left along the ridge. The trail,
sometimes a bit faded, goes along the right side of these remaining shrubs,
and then continues on top of the ridge after the last tree growth disappears.
Occasional rock cairns help mark the way. On the left are steep drop-offs
into a rocky basin below as the trail climbs up fairly steeply over the
boulders and loose rock.

At about 12,000 feet elevation the ridge bends to the right and leads up to a
false summit—a couple of very rocky knolls (marked as 12,453 feet on the

map) with severe drop-offs down to the right (north). From here you lose about 150 feet in elevation before making the final ascent up the ridge to the first of the two Sopris summits. On the south side of the summit is a nice grassy/tundra area and on the north side is a very steep drop into the basin below.

For the climb to the West Sopris summit descend 300 feet in elevation to the saddle to the west and then continue up to the second summit. During this entire trip you should keep your eyes on the sky and head back down as soon as you see any signs of imminent bad weather.

The twin peaks of 12,953-foot Mount Sopris in the Roaring Fork Valley.

Aspen to Crested Butte

One of the most popular hiking trips in the Central Colorado area is the hike between Aspen and Crested Butte over the Elk Mountain Range. The Victorian town of Crested Butte originated at the same time as Aspen during the mining boom over 100 years ago, but Crested Butte has resisted much of the change which Aspen has undergone. The quaintness and low-key environment of Crested Butte continues to attract visitors who need a break from the hustle and bustle of Aspen.

Automobile travelers have to take a long circuitous trip over Kebler Pass to get to Crested Butte from Aspen. Mountain bikers and four-wheel drive vehicles can make it over the rough Pearl Pass Road or Taylor Pass Road—when they are open. Hikers have the choice of three routes through the Maroon Bells-Snowmass Wilderness.

The hike to Crested Butte can be done in a day using Route #13, if the start is early and the hiker is strong. This 11-mile hike over West Maroon Pass comes out on the Schofield Pass Road about 14 miles from Crested Butte, necessitating making arrangements to get a ride for the final stretch. Routes #14 & #15 come out in Gothic, located about 7 miles north of Crested Butte; it's usually easy to get a ride from Gothic to Crested Butte. Some hikers do the 16-mile trip to Gothic via East Maroon Creek (Route #14) in one day, but camping near East Maroon Pass or at Copper Lake is the preferable alternative. Route #15 up Conundrum Creek is longer and more difficult, but it also is the most scenic and interesting of the three routes.

13. West Maroon Pass/Schofield Pass Road

Start/Destination: Maroon Lake/Schofield Pass Road (9,580/10,410 feet)
One-way Distance/Hiking Time: 11 miles/7 hours
Elevation Range: 9,580–12,500 feet
Maps: p. 38; USGS Maroon Bells, Snowmass Mountain; TI #128
Wilderness Designation: Maroon Bells-Snowmass Wilderness

General Comments: Going over West Maroon Pass is the shortest route to Crested Butte in terms of hiking, but it does involve getting a ride from the East Fork Trailhead at the Schofield Pass Road through Gothic to Crested Butte, a distance of about 14 miles. Most people make prior arrangements to have a taxi (Town Taxi in Crested Butte) or a friend pick them up at the trailhead; you can also try to hitchhike if you are so inclined, but there is virtually no traffic for the first couple of miles.

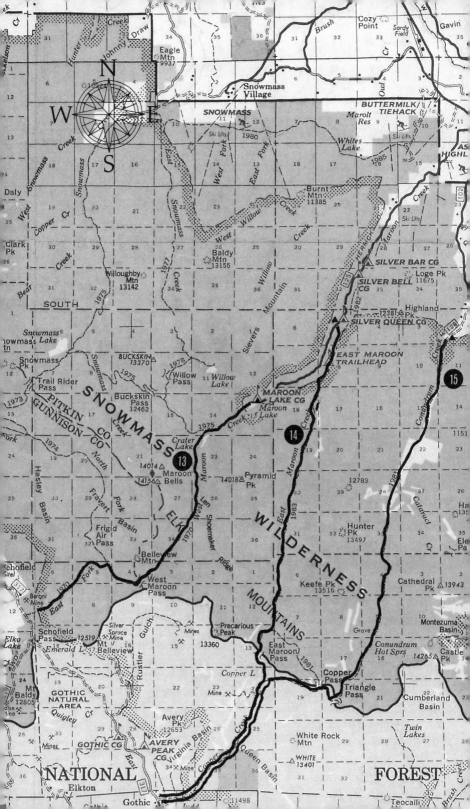

The hiking route involves about 3,000 feet of elevation gain through the West Maroon Valley to the spectacular West Maroon Pass (12,500 feet). It is best to start early in the day to avoid the early afternoon thunderstorms which are frequently encountered in the area of the pass. On the other side of the pass lie the most colorful fields of wildflowers in the Maroon Bells-Snowmass Wilderness.

If this trip is done as an overnight trip, rather than a day trip, it is best to camp before West Maroon Pass in one of the last small groves of trees before entering the tundra. No more sheltered camping sites exist until you get close to the Schofield Pass Road.

Directions to Trailhead: (Same as Route #4)

Trail Route: (Follow Route #4 to West Maroon Pass.) After taking a little time to rest and enjoy the views from the top of West Maroon Pass, continue down the switchbacks on the other side of the pass. As the trail descends into the valley you will encounter magnificent fields of wildflowers.

About a mile from the pass, when you come to an intersection with a trail going right to Frigid Air Pass, stay straight ahead on the main trail through the valley toward Schofield. Your route will take you through more fields of wildflowers and some scrub willow, as the trail follows the curve of the valley to the left. Just after crossing a small side stream about a mile from the trail junction, another trail heads right toward Hasley Basin. Continue left down the valley through more beautiful meadows with wildflowers.

In another two-thirds of a mile an indistinct trail breaks off to the left and crosses the East Fork (a shortcut to Schofield Pass through the trees). However, to get to the trailhead, stay straight on the main trail which ascends for a little distance through sloping meadows on the right side of the valley before descending again. At the next trail intersection continue going straight ahead down the valley. After a couple of downhill switchbacks the trail rounds the ruins of an old cabin. Follow the footpath down into the trees, and in five minutes, after going along the right side of the creek, you will come to the parking area and trailhead at the Schofield Pass Road.

If you are trying to catch a ride, head left on the dirt road toward Schofield Pass (10,707 feet), past Emerald Lake, and on to Gothic (about 7 miles). A lot of people visit Emerald Lake, so it should be easier to catch a ride at that point. From Gothic it is about 7 more miles to Crested Butte.

14. East Maroon Pass/Gothic

Start/Destination: East Maroon Trailhead/Gothic (8,680/9,600 feet)
One-way Distance/Hiking Time: 16 miles/2 days
Elevation Range: 8,680–11,820 feet
Maps: p. 38; USGS Highland Peak, Maroon Bells, Gothic; TI #128, 131
Wilderness Designation: Maroon Bells-Snowmass Wilderness

General Comments: The trail over East Maroon Pass is the most direct route to Crested Butte, but requires more hiking time than the West Maroon route. A few people make this trip in one day, but it is highly recommended to take a full two days and camp near East Maroon Pass. The camping is good in the trees before the pass; if you can make it to Copper Lake on the other side of the pass, you will have one of the prettiest places to camp in the entire wilderness.

Taking this route still involves getting a ride from Gothic to Crested Butte, but there are usually plenty of people willing to give you a lift. This route is mostly wooded and especially good in the fall when the aspen have turned color. See Route #2 for more information on the East Maroon Valley.

Directions to Trailhead: (Same as Route #2)

Trail Route: (Follow the trail route for Route #2 which will take you to the first of two stream crossings.) The chances are that you will not be able to make either stream crossing without getting your feet wet. Earlier in the summer when East Maroon Creek is high, the crossings will probably be impassable. The second crossing is one-half mile beyond the first. From here on you will be climbing steadily, mostly through old forests of spruce and fir with occasional views of the peaks ahead at the end of the valley.

In a little over two miles from the second stream crossing you will pass the Conundrum Trail which forks off to the left. Just beyond this junction is a stream cascading down through the rocks. Head to the right, cross the stream, and continue staying right on the main trail as a couple of false trails go off to the left. Finally, after contouring and meandering to the right for almost a mile, the trail curves up to the left and traverses uphill through a rockslide area to the pass. East Maroon Pass is marked by a sign in a small tundra area with scattered scrub growth and wildflowers.

As you head down the other side of the pass you will see Copper Lake below and White Rock Mountain in the background. Copper Lake is in a beautiful setting with a basin above it to the west, a few trees and knolls around the lake harboring camping sites, Copper Creek rushing down a gully below the lake, and rocky mountains encircling the lake.

On drawing even with Copper Lake you will come to a trail junction. A branch of the Conundrum Trail goes left to Triangle Pass; a trail goes down to the lake on your right; the main trail to Gothic and Crested Butte goes straight ahead. Stay straight on the main trail, an old jeep trail which starts dropping quite steeply, passing another branch of the Conundrum Trail after one-half mile. Follow the jeep trail down the drainage as other spurs veer off to the sides. After several easy creek crossings you will be in the open stream valley and soon the roaring creek descending through a deep canyon off to the left will signal your approach to Judd Falls.

Hiking the well-worn East Maroon Trail on the way to Crested Butte.

A little over 4 miles from Copper Lake you will come to a trail register and the Wilderness boundary with Judd Falls off to the left below you. The gate across the road blocks off access to private property ahead and the trail turns right toward the trailhead. Initially the trail goes up into the aspen, then contours up and down a little about one-half mile to the trailhead at the upper parking lot. From here it is a little over one-half mile down a dirt road to the lower parking lot on the Schofield Pass Road. Going left on this road brings you into Gothic and on to Crested Butte.

15. Conundrum/Triangle Pass/Gothic

Start/Destination: Conundrum Creek Trailhead/Gothic (8,760/9600 feet)
Round-trip Distance/Hiking Time: 19 miles/ 2 days
Elevation Range: 8,760–12,900 feet
Maps: p. 38; USGS Hayden Peak, Maroon Bells, Gothic; TI #127, #128, #131
Wilderness Designation: Maroon Bells-Snowmass Wilderness

General Comments: The Conundrum route to Crested Butte is the longest of the three in the guide, but undoubtedly the most interesting. The main attractions are the Conundrum Hot Springs in the beautiful Conundrum Creek Valley, the spectacular 12,900-foot Triangle Pass, Copper Pass (a 5-minute side trip), Copper Lake (another side trip), and White Rock Mountain. With a climb of over 4,000 feet to Triangle Pass and a distance of 19 miles to Gothic, this trip cannot be done in one day.

The two good areas for camping along the way are:(1) Near the Conundrum Hot Springs. However, this area is usually very crowded, so it's preferable to take a dip and then continue over Triangle Pass if the weather is good and you have the time. (2) At Copper Lake. This lake, with White Rock Mountain in the background, is a beautiful spot to camp, and is well worth taking the short side trip to get there.

Directions to Trailhead: From Highway 82 turn south one-half mile west of Aspen onto Castle Creek Road toward Ashcroft. Five miles up the road turn right onto Conundrum Road and follow this gravel road 1.1 miles to the parking area at the trailhead. Be careful not to go up any of the private drives along this road.

Trail Route: At the beginning of the hike, Hayden Peak looms ahead on the left. The ridge of peaks forming the valley wall beyond Hayden Peak consist of three peaks averaging over 14,000 feet—Cathedral Peak, Conundrum Peak, and Castle Peak.

Copper Lake with White Rock Mountain in the background.

For the first part of the hike the trail follows a jeep trail along the left side of Conundrum Creek. At 2½ miles you will make the first of three stream crossings over Conundrum Creek on a couple of large logs and continue on a foot trail. After a gradual ascent through forests, meadows, and avalanche slide debris the trail crosses the creek again at 6 miles, skirts around a round pond (Silver Dollar Pond), and passes several more beaver ponds just before the third stream crossing in the conifers at 6½ miles. This third crossing can be tricky—the high slanted log is often slick; it's best to go to the right and cross over a large log jam. Shortly before reaching the hot springs the trail runs alongside a small but deep rock canyon on the left. When you come to a cabin, look for the hot springs 200 yards beyond it on the other (left) side of the creek.

Beyond the hot springs, the trail continues along the right side of the creek, leaving the trees and climbing more steeply. With rocky peaks and reddish ridges in the background the trail, marked by occasional rock cairns, switchbacks up somewhat steeply and meanders through the tundra and fields of wildflowers. More switchbacks and a final traverse to the right take you up the final ascent to the rocky Triangle Pass. On the other side of the pass you can see the Copper Creek drainage straight ahead and Copper Pass close by on the right.

The trail continues over Triangle Pass to the left at first, and then cuts back to the right through scree toward Copper Pass. In about three-quarters of a mile you will pass a trail leading up to the right to Copper Pass (12,560 feet). A five-minute side trip up this trail will give you a look over the top into the East Maroon Valley. As you continue down the trail toward Copper Lake and Gothic, you will be traversing mostly over rock and rockslides along the right side of the valley.

About 1½ miles from the Copper Pass turnoff you will enter the woods and immediately come to a trail junction with a sign indicating that the right fork leads to Copper Lake and East Maroon Pass. (From here it is less than 10 minutes to Copper Lake.) To keep on the route to Gothic at this trail junction, stay straight and you will drop steeply through a picturesque setting with tall spruce and lush vegetation on the forest floor. In 10–15 minutes, after a steady descent, you will encounter the Copper Creek Trail (a jeep trail) descending from Copper Lake. Follow the jeep trail down the drainage as other spurs veer off to the sides. After several easy creek crossings you will be in the open stream valley and soon the roaring creek descending through a deep canyon off to the left will signal your approach to Judd Falls.

At Judd Falls, a little over 4 miles from Copper Lake, you will come to a trail register and the wilderness boundary. The gate across the road blocks off access to the private property ahead and the trail turns right toward the trailhead. Initially the trail goes up into the aspen, then contours up and down a little about one-half mile to the trailhead at the upper parking lot. From here it is a little over one-half mile down a dirt road to the lower parking lot on the Schofield Pass Road. Going left on this road brings you into Gothic and on to Crested Butte.

Independence Pass

The once rough road crossing the Continental Divide at Independence Pass (12,095 feet) was the main route between Leadville and Aspen for prospectors and settlers in the late 1800s. The ghost town of Independence, where gold was discovered on July 4, 1879, lies along this road several miles west of Independence Pass. Today the trip on the paved Highway 82 over the pass is one of the most spectacular drives on a paved road in Colorado. Highway 82 opens up the way from both the east and the west to many scenic high-altitude hikes in the tundra.

For those interested in learning more about the outdoors without having to expend much energy hiking, the Braille Trail (Route #16) combines a short experiential hike with the beautiful drive. The somewhat rough but very scenic Lincoln Creek Road leads from Highway 82 to Routes #17 & #18. Four-wheel drive is needed to get to the trailhead for Route #17 which takes you to two high alpine lakes. Route #18 follows Tabor Creek up a beautiful wildflower-filled valley and is somewhat easier to reach. If you wish to hike along the ridge of the Continental Divide to over 13,000 feet, try Route #19. The hike to Blue Lake, Route #20, is quite steep, but very picturesque as it climbs alongside a rushing, waterfall-filled creek.

Looking along the Continental Divide from Independence Pass.

16. Braille Trail

Start/Destination: Braille Trail Parking Lot (10,400 feet)
Round-trip Distance/Hiking Time: ¼ mile/one hour
Elevation Range: 10,400 feet
Maps: p. 46; USGS New York Peak; TI #127
Wilderness Designation: Non-Wilderness

General Comments: This self-guided nature trail in a spruce/fir forest is designed for the blind, but is also a wonderful educational experience for children and adults. A guide wire connects 22 stations which have texts in Braille and in print with information on the special outdoor experience at each station. Brochures about the trail and the stations are available at the beginning of the trail.

The Braille Trail was established in 1967 when it was the first of its kind anywhere in the world. The sighted can walk the trail with eyes closed or open, but probably would benefit the most by doing the trail first with eyes closed, then with eyes open.

Directions to Trailhead: Take Highway 82 southeast from Aspen for 12 miles (.8 miles past the 53-mile marker) to a gravel road and small parking circle for the trailhead on the right. A sign for the Braille Trail is posted about 1,000 feet before the turnoff.

Trail Route: The trail starts at the parking lot and follows a route over glacial moraine and through forest and meadow right near the Roaring Fork River. The distance between stations is anywhere from a few feet to over 100 feet.

Here is the description at a typical station: Station #5:"Within your reach are the branches of the Engelmann Spruce and the subalpine fir tree. The spruce needles are sharp and rigid and feel four-sided. The fir needles are flat and blunt. Both have characteristic smells. To remember fir from spruce, think of soft as fir to the touch. These needles are shed continually all year round, but so few at a time that the trees are always green."

Other subjects discussed and experienced at the stations include the following: timberline, the Roaring Fork River, squirrels and other small mammals, the juniper bush, needles and soil, growth rings on a stump, tree bark, lichen and fungus, rotting trees, peat moss, wound in trunk of a tree caused by a porcupine, river stones, willow and birch leaves, lodgepole pine, and plant life. After completing a fairly level loop the trail ends up back at the parking lot.

17. Anderson/Petroleum Lakes

Start/Destination: Petroleum Lake Trailhead/Petroleum Lake (11,200/12,300 feet)
Round-trip Distance/Hiking Time: 4 miles/3–4 hours
Elevation Range: 11,200–12,300 feet
Maps: p. 46; USGS New York Peak, Independence Pass; TI #127
Wilderness Designation: Non-Wilderness

General Comments: Anderson and Petroleum Lakes are located a mile apart above timberline in the tundra, surrounded by rocky knolls and peaks. The hike through the woods, meadows, and tundra abounds with wildflowers and the drive is as picturesque as the hike. The Lincoln Creek Road follows a cascading stream to Grizzly Reservoir, beyond which the road passes through a beautiful mountain valley. Past the reservoir the road can only be driven by high clearance four-wheel drive vehicles. All others will have to park and hike (or bike) from the Portal Campground by Grizzly Reservoir, which adds about 6 miles to the round trip.

Directions to Trailhead: Take Highway 82 southeast from Aspen 10 miles (just past mile marker 51) to Lincoln Creek Road on the right, drive up this somewhat bumpy road for 6.2 miles to Grizzly Reservoir and to the Portal Campground beyond. Here a sign indicates the road is "Rough, four-wheel drive only" and it means it. Three miles from the campground, exactly 10.0 miles from when you first turned onto Lincoln Creek Road, you will come to a main fork in the road (.4 mile beyond an old cabin on the left side of the road and .2 mile beyond another indistinct road off to the right). Take this right, go across the creek, and park on the other side.

Trail Route: The entire route follows an old jeep road, so it's hard to lose the way. The trail passes an old cabin on the right and climbs through the fir to the right of Anderson Creek. Two gates block the way to vehicles. At about one-half mile into the hike, still accompanied by the cascading creek, you will start seeing the rocky peaks jutting up ahead. After passing another cabin, the trail enters the tundra and soon forks to the left to Anderson Lake which sits in a little basin against the rocky backdrop.

To get to Petroleum Lake follow the branch of the jeep road to the right as it goes up through the tundra and wildflowers, contours around the rock faces off to the left, and stays left of the prominent Larson Peak. After passing by a pond on the right, you will see the outlet stream tumbling down from Petroleum Lake. Stay on the very steep path to the right of the stream to get to the lake. If you have extra time, try exploring the area beyond the lake with its interesting rocky knolls, little basins, and overlooks.

18. Tabor Creek Trail

Start/Destination: Tabor Creek Trailhead/Tabor Pass (10,240/12,460 feet)
Round-trip Distance/Hiking Time: 8 miles/6 hours
Elevation Range: 10,230–12,460 feet
Maps: p. 46; USGS New York Peak; TI #127
Wilderness Designation: Collegiate Peaks Wilderness

General Comments: This hike, mainly a pleasant walk up a classic U-shaped valley through meadows of flowers and across avalanche gullies, involves a few trail-finding skills for the last part of the route where the trail fades into the tundra. The destination at the end of the valley is a 12,460-foot pass which looks out into the basin containing Anderson and Petroleum lakes (see Route #17). The hike can include an optional side trip to Tabor Lake.

Directions to Trailhead: Take Highway 82 southeast from Aspen 10 miles (just past mile marker 51) to Lincoln Creek Road on the right. Go 4.2 miles up the bumpy Lincoln Creek Road to the Tabor Creek Trailhead on the right, located at the beginning of an open area exactly one mile past the New York Creek Trailhead.

Trail Route: The trail starts on an old jeep trail down to Lincoln Creek where it's necessary to cross either on a log or by wading. On the other side, the trail heads up into the trees quite steeply, first alongside an old stream gully, then above the steep-walled gully containing Tabor Creek. At one-half mile you will cross an aqueduct (New York Collection Canal) on a wooden bridge. The trail follows the roaring stream in the woods for one-third mile, then crosses the stream and breaks out into the open valley.

The trip through the valley is pleasant as you encounter gullies with some snow still remaining from the winter avalanches, meadows with a variety of wildflowers, and occasional spruce and fir trees. At about 2 miles into the hike, while going through the conifers, the trail crosses an open wet area full of wildflowers with water flowing down and a waterfall coming through the rocks above. This is the outlet stream from Tabor Lake which is located about 1,000 feet in elevation above the trail. If the lake is your destination, you can get there via some steep bushwhacking to the right of the wet area, but I would advise staying on the trail toward the pass. The Tabor Creek Trail continues to climb through the scattered conifers into the alpine tundra as the valley starts narrowing down.

As the hiking trail starts to fade in the tundra and a number of animal trails appear, make note of landmarks for your return trip and follow any rock cairns you might see, generally staying to the right of the headwaters of the stream and the marshy delta at the end of the creek. You will be making a couple of easy creek crossings as the creek bows out to the right. The last part of the route is a climb through a wide basin toward the saddle, mostly through grassy tundra, and then up through some rocks to the pass.

On the other side of the pass you will see Galena Creek, which flows into Lincoln Creek. The jagged mountain with a double peak is Larson Peak, beyond which lies the basin containing Anderson and Petroleum lakes. Off to the left is a mountainside streaked with red and orange from mining, above the ghost town of Ruby.

Looking from the Divide into the Grizzly Creek Valley toward Grizzly Peak.

19. Continental Divide

Start/Destination: Independence Pass/Peak 13,045 (12,095/13,045 feet)
Round-trip Distance/Hiking Time: 4 miles/3–4 hours
Elevation Range: 12,095–13,045 feet
Maps: p. 46; USGS Independence Pass; TI #127
Wilderness Designation: Collegiate Peaks Wilderness

General Comments: The Continental Divide is a string of summits of Rocky Mountain peaks that separates the streams flowing toward the Gulf of California and the Pacific Ocean to the west from those flowing toward the Gulf of Mexico and the Atlantic Ocean to the east. This particular route on the Continental Divide offers the hiker with a limited amount of time or experience the opportunity to hike to over 13,000 feet and see many of the 14,000-foot peaks of Central Colorado. Access to the trailhead is by a paved highway that winds up to the Divide from Aspen (to the west), and from Twin Lakes (to the east); this drive alone is an adventure.

The hiker should realize that the entire hike is over 12,000 feet and oxygen is quite sparse, so be prepared to go slowly. It is best to do the hike early in the day—afternoon thunderstorms are common at this elevation. The ridge is wide enough to be easy to hike, but some of the drop-offs along the latter part of the trail might affect those with a fear of heights. Great care should also be taken to stay on the trail so as not to impact the very fragile tundra. Alpine tundra wildflowers are abundant along the ridge.

Directions to Trailhead: The Independence Pass parking lot is located on Highway 82 about 20 miles east of Aspen, .2 mile past the 61-mile marker, right on the Continental Divide. From Leadville, take Highway 24 south to Highway 82 which you will take west through Twin Lakes to Independence Pass, a total distance of about 40 miles from Leadville.

Trail Route: From the parking lot at Independence Pass you can see the Continental Divide ridge extending to the west and south. About 100 yards up the path from the parking lot follow the old jeep trail on the right leading toward the ridge. During this gradual ascent, off to the west you will begin to see the 14,000-foot peaks of the Elk Mountain Range. After almost a mile you will be starting your climb up the ridge toward the first peak, Peak 12,812; the second peak on the ridge will be your goal. Half an hour or so of steady climbing will get you to the nice flat area on top of the first peak.

From here the trail descends a little before climbing to the next peak. Both sides of the trail, especially the left, are marked by steep drop-offs. The ghost town of Independence can be seen in the distance down to the right. Soon the ridge becomes very rocky as you ascend the last section along the right side of the ridge. The summit of Peak 13,045 is marked by a small rock shelter and a rock monument. Grizzly Peak (13,988 feet) looms ahead; the Grizzly Creek Valley is to the south and the Lincoln Creek Valley lies off to the west. Take time to look around—often you can see a herd of Rocky Mountain goats grazing on the flanks of the next peak on the divide, Peak 13,198. Return via the same route.

20. Blue Lake

Start/Destination: North Fork Lake Creek Trailhead/Blue Lake (10,880/12,495 feet)
Round-trip Distance/Hiking Time: 4 miles/4 hours
Elevation Range: 10,880–12,495 feet
Maps: p. 53; USGS Independence Pass, Mount Champion; TI #127
Wilderness Designation: Mount Massive Wilderness

General Comments: This very steep hike takes you along a beautiful, cascading stream and through a large, wildflower-filled valley to Blue Lake, tucked in against the mountains. The trail is not maintained by the Forest Service, and the latter portion fades into the tundra, thus requiring a few orienteering skills. You will not get lost, however, since the route follows the outlet stream from Blue Lake. The cascading stream and waterfalls in the woods during the first part of the hike make this one of the most picturesque routes in the area.

Directions to Trailhead: Take Highway 82 to mile marker 66 which is 4.8 miles east of Independence Pass and 19.3 miles west of Highway 24. Turn onto the dirt road on the east side of Highway 82 (on the valley floor near the switchback turn in Highway 82). Drive in .1 mile and park. (If you have a good four-wheel drive vehicle you can drive a little farther.) Cross the water flowing across the road and walk up the very rough road, staying to the left of the main stream. The road ends as it makes a loop on a steep hill and the trail goes off from the left end of the loop.

Trail Route: The trail starts up a beautiful valley above the roaring North Fork Lake Creek. In about one-quarter mile, just after crossing through a meadow with lots of wildflowers, you come to a creek (the outlet stream from Blue Lake), the Wilderness boundary, and a trail register. The trail forks here—you will have to stay left to get to Blue Lake; going straight ahead will take you up the valley. Cross the stream, stay along the right side, and head uphill. At first there may be no visible path, but after about 100 feet you will see the trail going off to the right into the woods.

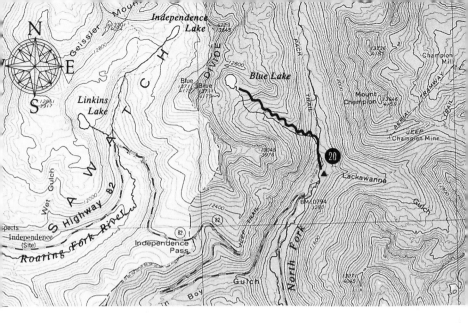

Follow the trail as it winds steeply up along the right side of the cascading stream. In spots the way may be blocked by fallen trees, and at times you will have to climb hand-over-foot because of the steepness. At about 11,650 feet elevation you will emerge from the woods into a valley bounded by peaks and rocky ridges. You will continue on a steady ascent as the trail traverses along the right side of the valley. When the trail fades away in the meadows and marshy areas, be sure to make note of a landmark so that you can pick up the trail more easily on the return trip.

To continue, keep on a steady ascending contour on the right side of the valley. Ahead in the center of the valley you will see huge smooth rocks on a somewhat steep mound. Go up the gully just along the right side of the rocks, stay to the right of the outlet stream, and you will come over a slight ridge with the lake tucked in behind in a cirque. The fishing is good, picnic spots are abundant, and expect to see some marmots and pika.

The beautiful cascading Blue Lake outlet stream.

Leadville

The historic town of Leadville, home of the Tabor Opera House and the Mining Hall of Fame, lies on the east side of the Continental Divide. This boom town of the 1870s and 1880s is now surrounded by abandoned silver mines and shadowed by 14,000-foot peaks. To the west of Leadville is Colorado's tallest mountain, Mount Elbert (see Routes #24–26), and Mount Massive, probably Colorado's largest mountain. In the shadow of these two peaks is the large Turquoise Lake, a major attraction for campers and fishermen.

Many high-altitude lakes on the east slope of the Continental Divide are popular destinations for either day or overnight hikes. The hike to Timberline Lake (Route #21) starts at the west end of Turquoise Lake. Hagerman Pass Road, which heads from Turquoise Lake over the Continental Divide into the Fryingpan River Valley, accesses a number of high altitude hikes, probably the most beautiful being the hike to Native Lake (Route #22). The longer hike (Route #23) to Willis Lake, which lies at the base of 13,933-foot Mount Hope, originates in the Twin Lakes area between Leadville and Independence Pass.

21. Timberline Lake

Start/Destination: Timberline Lake Trailhead/Timberline Lake (10,020/10,855 feet)
Round-trip Distance/Hiking Time: 4½ miles/3–4 hours
Elevation Range: 10,020–10,855 feet
Maps: p. 56; USGS Homestake Reservoir; TI #126
Wilderness Designation: Holy Cross Wilderness

General Comments: This pleasant, easy hike takes you to a beautiful lake surrounded by trees and the rocky ridges of the Continental Divide. The forest floor around the lake has lush vegetation and is full of needles, fallen trees, and decaying wood. Timberline Lake is an ideal spot to picnic, fish (catch & release), walk around and explore, or camp.

Directions to Trailhead: From Leadville take West 6th Street west from the center of town and follow signs to Turquoise Lake Recreation Area to pick up the route on the south side of the lake as described below.

From Aspen take Highway 82 east over Independence Pass to Highway 24 (44 miles from Aspen). Go left on Highway 24 toward Leadville; in 11.2

miles turn left on Road 300 toward Turquoise Lake. In .4 miles turn right on the road with a sign for Turquoise Lake. In 2.0 miles turn left on the paved road at the intersection by a commercial campground. In 1.0 miles where Turquoise Drive goes right, stay straight on Road 105 which will take you over the dam and around the south end of Turquoise Lake. Five miles from the dam you will come to a small parking area on the left by a stream (.3 miles past May Queen Campground entrance, just as the road makes a large curve to the right). Park here—the trailhead is just a couple of hundred feet to the west on the other side of the stream.

Trail Route: From the parking area walk to the right and cross immediately over the stream on your left to get to the trail register in the open area 200 feet west of the parking lot. Follow the old jeep trail to the left from the trail register and along the right side of the stream for 100 yards to a bridge over the stream. On the other side follow the jeep trail up along the left side of the stream. About 150 feet from the bridge where the Colorado Trail forks off to the left, stay straight on the jeep trail which you will be following all the way to Timberline Lake.

In about one-half mile you will be able to see the rocky ridges ahead. In another two-thirds mile, after wandering gradually through meadows and scattered trees, you will reach the first stream crossing. From here the trail gets a little steeper as you climb mostly through meadows, boulders, and wildflowers. In another one-half mile you will cross the stream again and make the last somewhat steep climb that takes you to the lake.

Timberline Lake at the foot of the Continental Divide.

Looking down at Native Lake with Mount Massive in the background.

22. Native Lake

Start/Destination: Trailhead on Hagerman Pass Road/Native Lake (10,800–11,220 feet)
Round-trip Distance/Hiking Time: 7 miles/5 hours
Elevation Range: 10,800–11,860 feet
Maps: p. 56; USGS Mount Massive; TI #127 (#126 is helpful)
Wilderness Designation: Mount Massive Wilderness

General Comments: Flanked by the Continental Divide and set at the base of 14,421-foot Mount Massive, Native Lake is one of the area's best destinations for a day hike and offers a magnificent place to pitch a tent for backpackers. I would recommend taking the extra time to camp here so that you can enjoy all the beauty and places to explore that this location offers. However, this route can easily be done as a day hike if you get an early start. Wildlife, especially deer, will frequently be seen along the trail.

The hike itself is extremely pleasant, with the trail switchbacking back and forth across a stream through a peaceful wooded setting before reaching a plateau with views of Leadville below. The final descent to Native Lake with Mount Massive looming behind the lake should provide good photo opportunities. If the weather turns bad, cover can be found among some large rocks on the east side of the lake which form a cave-like shelter.

Directions to Trailhead: From Leadville take West 6th Street west from the center of town and follow signs to Turquoise Lake Recreation Area to pick up route on south side of lake as described below. From Aspen take Highway 82 east over Independence Pass to Highway 24 (44 miles from Aspen). Go left on Highway 24 toward Leadville; in 11.2 miles turn left on Road 300 toward Turquoise Lake. In .4 miles turn right on the road with a sign for Turquoise Lake. In 2.0 miles turn left onto a paved road at the intersection by a commercial campground. In 1.0 miles where Turquoise Drive goes right, stay straight on Road 105 which will take you over the dam and around the south end of Turquoise Lake. Three miles past the dam you will come to Hagerman Pass Road, a gravel road on the left. Take this somewhat rough road 3.6 miles to a parking lot on the left (just before a big curve in the road to the right) where the trailhead is located.

Trail Route: The well-worn trail starts out in tall fir trees and gradually contours via long switchbacks up the side of the valley, making a number of easy stream crossings. In about 2 miles you will come to a plateau-like meadow where the trail is marked by posts supported by stones. Mount Massive sprawls out in front of you, and the valley with Leadville lies down to the left, backed by other 14,000-foot peaks. The trail passes by some ponds before starting down after one-half mile of mostly level terrain.

On the descent you can see Native Lake below in the trees. About one-half hour from the top you will arrive at the swampy end of the lake. If you're backpacking, camping is good at this end, but the best camping and prettiest area is on the other side. Go left (clockwise) around the lake to avoid having to cross a wet area and the outlet stream.

23. Willis Lake

Start/Destination: Willis Gulch Trailhead/Willis Lake (9,350/11,740 feet)
Round-trip Distance/Hiking Time: 11 miles/9 hours (or 2 days)
Elevation Range: 9,350–11,810 feet
Maps: p. 62; USGS Mount Elbert; TI #127
Wilderness Designation: Non-Wilderness

General Comments: It's possible to do this hike either as a long day trip or as a camping trip. Willis Lake is set in a cirque against rocky 13,933-foot Mount Hope in a valley bounded by almost a dozen 13,000-foot summits. A few open spots around the edge of the lake can be used to pitch a tent, but camping farther down the valley is preferable. Fishing in the lake is generally quite rewarding, and a side trip to the old mine which can be seen beyond the lake makes an interesting diversion.

Directions to Trailhead: From Leadville go 15 miles south on Highway 24 to Highway 82. Go right on Highway 82 for 8.6 miles to a gravel road turnoff on the left (south) side of the road. This turnoff is 35 miles east of Aspen on Highway 82 (.6 miles east of the Parry Peak Campground entrance). Go down this gravel road .1 miles to a parking area by the river. Continue on foot, cross the bridge over Lake Creek and go straight ahead on the trail to the far end of a beaver pond, about 200 feet from the bridge, where you will come to the trail register and the trail going off to the left.

If you are staying in the Parry Peak Campground, follow the road (by foot) through the campground over a bridge and stay left to a gate. Continue on the other side of the gate for about one-quarter mile to where the road turns into a path. Follow the path through the woods for the last couple of hundred feet to the trail register and the trail going off to the right.

Trail Route: Follow the trail as it contours around the beaver ponds and heads east up the mountainside. After a steep climb, watch for a fork in the trail about one-third mile from the trailhead. Take the right fork and continue on a contour up the mountain. The steep climb through mixed conifer, aspen, and rocks will take you to the abandoned Arlington Ditch which used to carry water from Lake Creek to the east. Stay left on the trail along the ditch in the aspen for about 10 minutes of pleasant, level hiking.

After crossing an earth slide area, you will approach Willis Gulch and a picturesque stream crossing. When the water is high in the spring you may have to cross a little further upstream. On the east side of the stream at the wide, well-worn Colorado Trail head up to the right. Make very careful note of this junction so as not to miss the turn on the way back. This section of trail which you will be following uphill through the woods is part of the annual Leadville 100-mile foot race and leads to Hope Pass.

In 15–20 minutes you will come to the junction with another well-worn trail that heads off to the right up Willis Gulch. Go right and follow this trail as it climbs gently through the tall conifers. In a couple of minutes you will cross the outlet stream for Little Willis Lake, and then in another 10–15 minutes you will have to cross Big Willis Creek. The trail continues along the right side of this beautiful cascading creek on a path strewn with pine needles. After almost a mile, the trail exits the woods into an open meadow, ascends into a huge rockslide area, and then meanders through willows, open clearings, and meadows covered by wildflowers.

During your hike up the valley you will pass the ruins of a couple old cabins and will see mine tailings and the ruins of several mine buildings on the hillside above you. About 10 minutes after passing a small lake, you will see the larger Willis Lake ahead. As you draw even with Willis Lake, the trail will drop steeply down to the lake, your destination.

Mount Elbert

Mount Elbert at 14,433 feet is the highest peak in Colorado and the second highest in the Continental U.S. Due to the relatively easy route for such a high peak, Mount Elbert is one of the most frequently climbed peaks in all of Colorado. The view from the summit is spectacular in every direction. However, only the physically fit and those acclimated to high altitude should attempt the hike—at over 14,000 feet the air is very thin, and climbing 4,000–5,000 feet of elevation is extremely demanding.

Some hikers climb to treeline, camp, and continue to the summit the next day, but most do the round trip in one day. It's very common for storms to appear quickly around noon at the peak, so ideally the hiker should summit before noon for an early start down. Campgrounds are strategically situated at the trailheads for camping the night before the trip up the mountain.

Dehydration is a problem at high altitudes, so carry plenty of water on the trip. Bring foul-weather gear in case you get caught in one of the sudden high-altitude storms, and be aware that it can be very cold and windy on the upper part of this hike.

Of the three major routes to the summit, the South and the North Mount Elbert trails (Routes #24 & #25) are the recommended routes. Neither involves treacherous trails or exposure. The South Trail is more accessible for hikers coming from Aspen and the North Trail is closer to Leadville. The Black Cloud Trail (Route #26), should only be attempted by serious, experienced hikers and climbers who have no fear of heights.

24. South Mount Elbert Trail

Start/Destination: Lakeview Campground/Mount Elbert (9,550/14,433 feet)
Round-trip Distance/Hiking Time: 11 miles/8–12 hours
Elevation Range: 9,550–14,433 feet
Maps: p. 62; USGS Mount Elbert, Granite; TI #127, 110
Wilderness Designation: Non-Wilderness

General Comments: The South Trail is the easiest and most used route up Mount Elbert. The starting point as described here is the official trailhead, although some hikers with four-wheel drive vehicles drive up the gravel road from the campground to get a higher start. For the first two miles of the hike you will be following the well-signed Colorado Trail.

Getting to treeline on the South Mount Elbert Trail with the summit ahead.

Directions to Trailhead: From Aspen take Highway 82 east for 38 miles to Twin Lakes. Beyond the community of Twin Lakes you will come to a large power plant and visitor center on the right side of the road. One-quarter mile past the power plant on the left side is a paved road which leads to Lakeview Campground.

To get to this road from Leadville, take Highway 24 south for 15 miles to Highway 82 and turn right. The turnoff to Lakeview Campground is in 4 miles on the right side of the road, one-quarter mile before the power plant. One mile up the paved road make a left turn into the campground. Turn left at the signboard onto a gravel road and follow signs to Loop H and the trailhead for Mount Elbert.

Trail Route: Walk the path up the hill through the sagebrush a couple of hundred yards to the gravel road and go left. You will be following this road and signs for the Colorado Trail through beautiful stands of aspen for almost 2 miles. When you come to the end of the road at a creek crossing, follow the foot trail on the other side over another trickle of water to get onto the trail on the left in the aspen.

In about 10 minutes, after a slight downgrade, you will come to a trail junction in the trees with a trail register. The Colorado Trail leaves you here and goes down to the right toward some ponds; you will be taking the Mount Elbert Trail up to the left. After a little less than a mile of steep climbing through beautiful groves of aspen the way starts opening up and you can see the defined ridge which you will be following to the summit. At about 11,700 feet you emerge into the open completely and start ascending a little more steeply again.

As you get higher up the route starts getting rockier and small alpine wildflowers are present everywhere. Be careful not to shortcut the trails which destroys the vegetation in the tundra. The rest of the way to the summit involves a steady climb. Only the altitude and lack of oxygen makes the hike difficult—there are no steep drop-offs and only a little loose rock. When getting close to the top, make sure to remember landmarks for the last part of your route for the return trip—it is very easy to become a little disoriented at the top and head down the wrong trail.

25. North Mount Elbert Trail

Start/Destination: Halfmoon Road/Mount Elbert (10,070/14,433 feet)
Round-trip Distance/Hiking Time: 10 miles/7–10 hours
Elevation Range: 10,070–14,433 feet
Maps: p. 62; USGS Mount Massive, Mount Elbert; TI #127
Wilderness Designation: Non-Wilderness

General Comments: The North Mount Elbert Trail is the shortest and quickest way to get to the summit of Mount Elbert, but getting to the trailhead requires 7 miles of driving on a gravel road. The trailhead is located by a campground, making it convenient to stay overnight for an early morning start. The North Mount Elbert Trail follows the northeast ridge to the summit and, like the South Mount Elbert Trail, is not extremely difficult or treacherous.

Directions to Trailhead: From Aspen drive 44 miles east on Highway 82 to Highway 24, go left for 11.2 miles to Road 300 and turn left. From Leadville go 4 miles south on Highway 24 and turn right onto Road 300.

Set your odometer at the intersection of Highway 24 and Road 300 and follow the signs toward Halfmoon Campground, which involves the following route: turn left onto a gravel road at .7 miles, turn right at 1.9 miles, at 6.0 miles continue past Halfmoon Campground, and at 7.2 miles you will reach the Elbert Creek Campground. This is a good place to camp, since the trailhead is only .3 miles ahead. At 7.5 miles, just before crossing the creek, you can see the trailhead to Mount Elbert in the woods on the left. If you are not camping, you can park just over the bridge on the right beyond the Mount Elbert Trailhead.

The author and friends on top of Colorado's highest peak.

Trail Route: The trail starts out following the Colorado Trail, initially heading gradually through the woods to the left. About 15 minutes into the hike you will pass the remains of an old cabin on the left. After a steady, steep climb away from Elbert Creek, the trail levels off a little and soon comes to a junction where the Colorado Trail stays to the left and the trail to Mount Elbert goes up to the right.

Go right on the Mount Elbert Trail which starts out as a pleasant walk through mostly pine trees, passing the old trail on the left which was blocked off in 1992 and rerouted up to the right on the ridge. From here you will continue to climb quite steeply for a while before the trail eases off as it reaches the top of the ridge and heads toward the visible summit ahead. At about 11,880 feet elevation you will break out of the trees into the open and can get a good look at the peak ahead.

You will be following the main ridge all the way to the top; it is not possible to get lost, your route and the summit ahead are in full view. After some steep climbing through open meadow and up switchbacks to regain the top of the main ridge, you simply continue along the rocky ridge through the tundra to the top. Inhale a little extra oxygen and check landmarks as you approach the summit so as not to head down the wrong trail on the return trip.

26. Black Cloud Trail

Start/Destination: Black Cloud Trailhead/Mount Elbert
(9,700/14,433 feet)
Round-trip Distance/Hiking Time: 11 miles/9–13 hours
Elevation Range: 9,700–14,433 feet
Maps: p. 62; USGS Mount Elbert; TI #127
Wilderness Designation: Non-Wilderness

General Comments: The Black Cloud Trail is not recommended for
general use to reach the summit of Mount Elbert. It is the most difficult and
treacherous of the three trails. In spots the trail is quite steep, the footing is
often quite poor, bad weather can make parts of the trail almost impassable,
and towards the top the exposure could affect those with any fear of heights.
Only serious, experienced hikers and climbers with good map-reading skills
should attempt this route.

Directions to Trailhead: From Leadville take Highway 24 south 15
miles to Highway 82. Turn left onto Highway 82 and go 11 miles (.7 miles
west of Twin Peaks Campground) to a gravel road on the right, which
should be marked by a small sign for the Black Cloud Trail. The trailhead is
right up this road. From Aspen travel 33 miles east on Highway 82 to the
gravel road on the left (.1 mile east of Mount Elbert Lodge).

Trail Route: Use the route as marked on the Trails Illustrated Map #127
and refer to the USGS Mount Elbert Quadrangle for greater detail. Bring an
altimeter and be sure to stay left at the trail junction at 11,020 feet. Be
especially careful of the poor footing.

Fryingpan River Valley

The Fryingpan River, one of the best trout streams in the country, originates at the Continental Divide and forms one of the most scenic and spectacular valleys in Central Colorado. The only paved road access to the valley is from the town of Basalt. The gravel, four-wheel drive Hagerman Pass Road from Leadville drops into the back end of the valley, but this road is only open for a short time during the summer when it is not blocked by snow.

Beyond Ruedi Reservoir (located 14 miles up the valley from Basalt) the Fryingpan River is fed by a multitude of streams flowing from high mountain lakes set in basins high above the valley floor. The hikes listed in this chapter cover a number of the trails to these lakes. These routes in the Fryingpan River Valley are generally not very heavily used, since the drive to the trailheads is about 30–40 miles from Highway 82.

Although most of the hikes in the valley can be done as day hikes, the Fryingpan River Valley is especially attractive to campers and backpackers. The many stream valleys and lakes set at timberline offer attractive settings and locations for campsites, and some excellent fishing. The tundra in the

Fryingpan Lakes—Two of the many lakes in the Fryingpan River Valley.

Fryingpan abounds with wildflowers and wildlife. Above timberline the rocky basins, cirques, ridges, and passes present unique opportunities for the backpacker to explore the high country on day trips from his campsite. It is possible to spend weeks in the Fryingpan River Valley and see new territory every day.

The road past Elk Wallow Campground, Road 501, leads to Routes #27 & #28. The short hike to Savage Lakes (Route #27) is one of the most popular hikes in the valley because of the spectacular setting of the lakes. The hike to Josephine Lake (Route #28) usually includes wildlife sightings and can be done as a day hike, but is best as an overnighter.

The Sawyer Lake route (Route #29) is a pleasant and relatively easy trip through the woods, one often taken by families and hikers who also want to do a little fishing. The trailhead for Lyle and Mormon Lakes (Route #30) is reached by driving up the Hagerman Pass Road, a dramatic trip by car before even starting the hike.

Route #31 involves another adventurous drive to a trail that takes you through a pleasant valley full of avalanche paths and wildflowers to three lakes located near the end of the Fryingpan River Valley, in a setting framed by the Continental Divide. The trip to Granite Lakes (Route #32) is longer and more difficult, and must be done as a backpack trip.

27. Savage Lakes

Start/Destination: Road 501/Savage Lakes (9,880/11,150 feet)
Round-trip Distance/Hiking Time: 4 miles/3 hours
Elevation Range: 9,880–11,150 feet
Maps: p. 68; USGS Nast; TI #126
Wilderness Designation: Holy Cross Wilderness

General Comments: The relatively short Savage Lakes Trail takes you to a pair of lakes at timberline with one of the finest wilderness settings in the Fryingpan River Valley. These two lakes, one set at about 100 feet higher elevation than the other, are nestled against a rocky basin and ridge, offering opportunities for further hiking, climbing, and exploration. The wooded hike to the lakes is scenic and pleasant, although fairly steep, following a gorgeous mountain stream winding through the forest. Good campsites exist at both lakes, with the upper lake being the better choice because of its higher elevation and spectacular setting. Camping is also available at Elk Wallow Campground, 5 miles before the trailhead.

Directions to Trailhead: From the intersection of Fryingpan Road (Midland Ave.) and old Highway 82 in Basalt drive 26.4 miles up the Fryingpan Road to a gravel road (Road 501) on the left just before the road crosses the river. Follow the gravel road 7.9 miles (stay left at the intersection at 4.5 miles) to the Savage Lakes Trailhead on the left. It takes about an hour to drive to the trailhead from Basalt.

Trail Route: The trail starts up the left side of the creek, climbing steadily through a beautiful conifer forest strewn with boulders. In a little less than a mile the trail levels off a little alongside the creek. Rocky cliffs and a boulder-strewn area lie off to the left, the trail is shaded by tall Douglas firs, and the cascading creek on the right creates numerous small waterfalls. The trail soon starts ascending more steeply.

About 200 yards before Lower Savage Lake a trail to Carter Lake goes off to the left. Stay right as the Savage Lakes Trail levels off and goes through a marshy meadow. You will soon see the lake ahead as you drop down to the shoreline through the trees. Several big rocks jutting out into the lake make good picnic sites. On the other side of the lake is a rocky ridge and the outlet stream from the upper lake flowing down through the rocks.

To continue on, go around the left side of Lower Savage Lake on a rocky trail. After about 5 minutes, at a split in the trail, stay left. In about 2–3 minutes, at the next fork, stay right and continue up over a short steep section to get to the overlook above the lower lake. From here it is only a couple of hundred feet along the outlet stream to the upper lake.

28. Josephine Lake

Start/Destination: Henderson Park Trailhead/Josephine Lake (9,240/11,380 feet)
Round-trip Distance/Hiking Time: 9 miles/8 hours or 2 days
Elevation Range: 9,240–11,560 feet
Maps: p. 68; USGS Nast, Mount Jackson; TI #126
Wilderness Designation: Holy Cross Wilderness

General Comments: Josephine Lake, tucked in against the rugged peaks of the Sawatch Range, is a great destination for a long day hike. However, the camping, exploring, fishing, and sights are so good at Josephine Lake, that I would advise making this a backpacking trip. Expect to observe wildlife such as elk, coyote, deer, grouse, porcupines, etc., on your way to the lake. You're also not likely to forget the panorama of peaks and valleys that are visible from ridge on the last part of the hike. Good side trips from the lake include a hike up to Savage Peak, and hikes up into the basin above the lake and to some of the rocky ridges beyond.

Directions to Trailhead: From the intersection of Fryingpan Road (Midland Ave.) and old Highway 82 in Basalt drive 26.4 miles up the Fryingpan Road to a gravel road (Road 501) on the left just before the road crosses the Fryingpan River. Follow the gravel road 4.5 miles (you will pass Elk Wallow Campground at 3.0 miles) to a fork in the road. Stay left on Road 501 (Cunningham Creek Road goes right), and in one-tenth of a mile on the left will be a small wooden sign (very easy to miss) for the Henderson Park Trailhead, Trail #1917.

Trail Route: The first part of the hike is a climb through aspen, grassy areas with wildflowers, and then beautiful woods of tall aspen with ferns on the forest floor. After about 1½ miles you will come to a large, sloped clearing full of wildflowers and other vegetation. A little beyond this clearing in the conifers, when you come to the trail junction with the Carter Basin Trail on your right, stay straight on the left side of the creek.

In a little over 100 yards from the trail junction you will reach the very flat open area of Henderson Park, a marshy meadow surrounded by conifers. Ahead you can see a long ridge leading to the barren Savage Peak, the ridge you will be climbing the last part of the hike. In Henderson Park the trail will probably not be evident. Stay left on the trail in the woods which follows the edge of the open area and then rises up away from the park. In about 10–15 minutes from Henderson Park the trail comes up over a little rise and drops down to another clearing, Coffeepot Park. Stay on the trail in the woods alongside the park. At the far end of the park, just as the trail heads away from the park, you will come to a trail intersection (easily missed) with wooden signs on a tree. The trail to Last Chance goes straight, while the trail to Josephine Lake goes to the right. Take the right as the trail gradually ascends, traversing the side of a ridge, and then climbs more steeply up the ridge through spruce and pine toward Savage Peak. After a beautiful walk up the ridge for about 1½ miles, you will come to a sign for Josephine Lake which lies below you to the left. The trail to the lake goes down the steep, north face of the ridge. The best camping spots are located in the trees and in the general vicinity of the outlet stream.

Josephine Lake as seen from the trail on the ridge above.

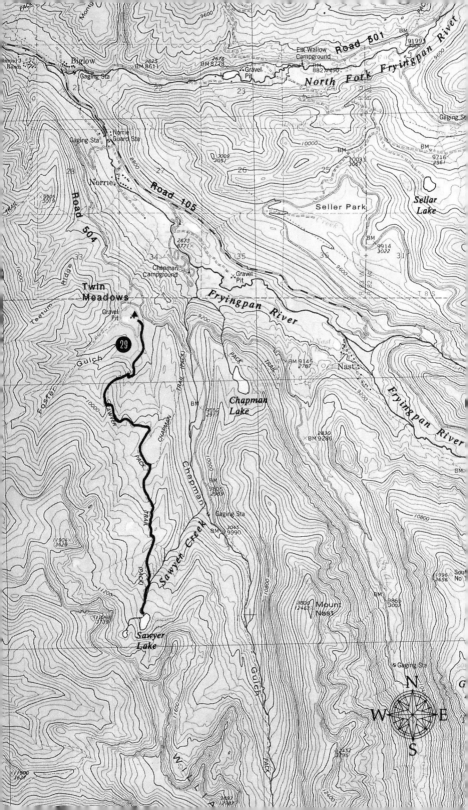

29. Sawyer Lake

Start/Destination: Twin Meadows/Sawyer Lake (9,460/11,020 feet)
Round-trip Distance/Hiking Time: 8 miles/6 hours
Elevation Range: 9,460–11,020 feet
Maps: p. 72; USGS Meredith, Thimble Rock; TI #126,127
Wilderness Designation: Hunter Fryingpan Wilderness

General Comments: The Sawyer Lake Trail is a good, mostly wooded day hike for a pleasant outing, or for some relaxed fishing. The trees surrounding the lake contain many good camping spots for those wishing to spend the night. The trail route passes through a variety of beautiful conifer forests and open areas with lots of wildflowers. Deer and elk are often seen along this route. It is also possible to get up to a second lake above Sawyer Lake, but no trail exists and the way is wet and cluttered by many fallen trees and undergrowth.

Directions to Trailhead: From the intersection of Fryingpan Road (Midland Ave.) and old Highway 82 in Basalt drive 27.5 miles up the Fryingpan Road to the Norrie turnoff. Turn right onto Road 504, a gravel road, and follow this road as it switchbacks and traverses up from the valley floor. At 3.4 miles take the right fork toward the Sawyer Lake Trail. Drive past the first trailhead (the Aspen-Norrie Trailhead) to the second trailhead at .4 miles at the end of the road in Twin Meadows and park.

Trail Route: From the parking lot follow the two tracks going along the left side of the stream in the meadow. As you enter the woods there will be a trail sign indicating that this is Sawyer Lake Trail #1926. The trail crosses several small streams in the woods and takes a gradual ascent through a forest of tall pines.

At 1 mile the well-worn trail starts ascending a little more steeply through the pine. As the trail levels off you will be passing through some clearings from where you can see the peaks ahead. After leaving the clearings, the trail enters a nice stand of tall fir trees, crosses a small stream, and starts climbing a little. At a little over 2 miles the route gets rougher and steeper through the woods before leveling out in a partially open area, passing some ponds, and descending to a stream crossing.

Eventually, after walking through some picturesque wooded areas, you will approach the outlet stream from the lake, cross the stream, and follow along its left side to a marshy area and Sawyer Lake. Stay left for campsites and places to fish and relax.

30. Lyle & Mormon Lakes

Start/Destination: Lyle Lake Trailhead/Mormon Lake
(10,720/11,460 feet)
Round-trip Distance/Hiking Time: 7 miles/4–5 hours
Elevation Range: 10,720–11,680 feet
Maps: p. 74; USGS Nast; TI #126
Wilderness Designation: Holy Cross Wilderness

General Comments: On this trip you may spend as much time driving
as hiking, but it's well worth the time. Not only is the hike beautiful and
scenic, so is the drive, especially on Hagerman Pass Road where you will be
overlooking the Fryingpan River Valley and Ivanhoe Creek from a road
bordered by steep drop-offs. This road can be driven with a two-wheel drive
vehicle, but four-wheel drive is preferred because of the rough road and a
couple of water crossings.

The hike to the first lake, Lyle Lake, is an easy hike through a broad tundra
valley. Many hikers stop at Lyle Lake, picnic or fish, and return to the
trailhead. However, the most beautiful and spectacular scenery lies between
Lyle Lake and Mormon Lake. This section is a real backcountry hike with a
variety of terrain, ending at a beautiful lake nestled up against a steep, rocky
ridge. With an early start you can have a great day hike to Mormon Lake
and back, but, if possible, plan on camping at Mormon Lake. You'll
probably see elk and other wildlife while you're there, and the fishing is
good.

Directions to Trailhead: From the intersection of Fryingpan Road
(Midland Ave.) and old Highway 82 in Basalt set your trip odometer and
drive up the paved Fryingpan Road. Stay on the main paved road past the
reservoir and along the Fryingpan River; at 32.1 miles you will come to a
gravel road on the right going to Fryingpan Lakes. Stay left on the
Hagerman Pass Road (Road 105) which curves around to the left and turns
to gravel just past this junction. At 35.6 miles stay straight on Road 105 as
you pass a road going left to Diemer and Sellar lakes. At 43.0 miles you
will come to the intersection with the Ivanhoe Lake Road. Go left up the
short hill on the Hagerman Pass Road for 200 feet to the Lyle Lake
Trailhead and parking.

Trail Route: The trail begins with a gradual climb through scattered trees
and lots of wildflowers, and continues through a tundra landscape in a broad
valley marked by a rocky ridge at the end. After a little over a mile of very
gradual ascent along the left side of the valley, the trail follows the curve of
the valley up to the left as it steepens on its final climb to Lyle Lake. A

The beauty and solitude of Morman Lake.

large grassy meadow lies in front on the lake; rocky cliffs and a rock slide area dominate the right side of the lake.

To continue to Mormon Lake, cross the outlet creek just before the lake and follow the trail along the right edge of Lyle Lake through a rock field. Occasional cairns will mark the way. As you get out of the big rocks and into the grass, watch for a trail fork and follow the trail ascending up to the right away from Lyle Lake. It will take you about 15 minutes to reach the ridge above the lake from where you can look back to the south and see Mount Massive and other peaks in the distance.

The trail continues on a contour along the slope of the mountain on the right, staying fairly level and passing through beautiful high country marked by rocks, wildflowers, scattered trees, and occasional streams coming down from the rocks above. Patches of snow often remain here until late in the summer. Although not heavily traveled, the trail is fairly distinct; however don't be misled by the side game trails.

After almost a mile you will see a barren, rocky divide ahead and come to a pond in a flat area. Stay right of the pond (the trail may not be evident here) and proceed toward Mormon Lake nestled below the sheer rock faces ahead. Follow the ridge that leads down to the lake and continue along the left side of the lake for good views, picnicking, and camping.

31. Fryingpan Lakes

Start/Destination: Road 505/Fryingpan Lakes (9,950/11,020 feet)
Round-trip Distance/Hiking Time: 9 miles/7 hours
Elevation Range: 9,950–11,020 feet
Maps: p. 74; USGS Mount Champion; TI #127
Wilderness Designation: Hunter Fryingpan Wilderness

General Comments: This route follows the Fryingpan River to three lakes—a lower lake and two Fryingpan Lakes. The source of the Fryingpan River lies just beyond the lakes below the ridge of the Continental Divide. This easy hike and the long drive to the trailhead, makes a good all-day trip or overnight camping trip. The 38-mile drive from Basalt up the Fryingpan River Valley alone is worth the trip, especially the last 6 miles on the gravel road traversing high up the side of the valley.

The trail to the lakes goes through a V-shaped valley, bounded on one side by the Continental Divide and on the other by almost a dozen summits over 13,000 feet. The treed valley walls are marked by avalanche chutes and waterfalls; the valley floor holds fields of wildflowers, boulders, and occasional debris from the winter avalanches. The trail to the lowest lake (10,900 feet) is easy to follow and does not pass through any difficult terrain. From that point on the way gets marshy, rocky, and steeper. The best camping sites are at the lowest of the three lakes.

Directions to Trailhead: From the intersection of Fryingpan Road (Midland Ave.) and old Highway 82 in Basalt drive up the paved Fryingpan Road. At 32.1 miles take a right on a gravel road to with a sign to Fryingpan Lakes. Drive 5.9 miles to the end of the road by the gaging station on the river and park on the left. The Fryingpan River (on your left) and Marten Creek (on your right) flow together at the gaging station. A small bridge crosses the Fryingpan, and leads to the trailhead on the other side.

Trail Route: The route ascends very gradually through a beautiful spruce and fir forest. After a mile the trail starts crossing avalanche paths as it periodically emerges into open areas. Watch for all the evidence of the winter avalanches—the debris, uprooted trees, and open vertical paths with trees along the edges at various stages of growth. The peak you see at the end of the valley is Deer Mountain (13,761 feet), and the one ahead on the left is Mount Oklahoma (13,845 feet), both on the Continental Divide.

A little over two miles into the hike you will cross a small log bridge over the creek and soon will enter some old growth forest. (Make note of the location of this stream crossing for your trip back.) Half an hour later, after passing through a beautiful meadow at the foot of a rockslide, you will find yourself at the bottom of a huge avalanche chute with only one surviving large tree. From here it's about 15–20 minutes to the lowest of the three lakes. The meadow before this lake is an ideal picnic spot.

Beyond this point the trail gets more difficult to follow as it passes through a rock field, and then in the woods beyond the lake through some muddy and marshy spots. The trail continues up along the left of the stream through a pretty bouldered area. It will take about 20– 25 minutes to hike to the first of the two Fryingpan Lakes from the lowest lake. The first Fryingpan Lake is surrounded by rocks; the second Fryingpan Lake lies just beyond the first over a small ridge. The north end of the second lake is shallow and marshy, but there are a few possible camp sites above the lake.

One of the many avalanche chutes above the Fryingpan Lakes Trail.

32. Granite Lakes

Start/Destination: Granite Lakes Trailhead/Granite Lakes
(8,762– 11,590 feet)
Round-trip Distance/Hiking Time: 12 miles/2–3 days
Elevation Range: 8,762–11,620 feet
Maps: p. 74; USGS Nast, Mount Champion; TI #126, 127
Wilderness Designation: Hunter Fryingpan Wilderness

General Comments: The first half of this hike ascends gently along the
Fryingpan River to Granite Creek. The second half follows a very steep,
rugged, and sometimes muddy trail along Granite Creek up to Granite
Lakes. The trail is occasionally used by pack trips from the guest ranch,
otherwise traffic is quite light. Many people end their hike and camp at
Lower Granite Lake. However, the adventurous with good map-reading
skills should continue on to the second lake and the solitude it offers. The
trail between the two lakes fades away, so attention to the map and trail
description is a must. Upper Granite Lake is set in an area that is home to
many elk. The basin at the end of the valley beyond the lake is very
picturesque, with lots of wildflowers, many good lookout points, and places
to explore. Fishing in both lakes is good.

Directions to Trailhead: From the intersection of Fryingpan Road
(Midland Ave.) and old Highway 82 in Basalt drive up the paved Fryingpan
Road. At 31.3 miles (3.8 miles past the Norrie turnoff) turn right at the road
with the sign for the Granite Lakes and Nast Lake trailheads. One mile
down the winding road you will come to the parking for the Nast Lake
Trailhead. Park here and walk .2 mile down the road to the Granite Lakes
Trailhead on the left at the guest ranch parking lot.

Trail Route: The trail follows a road for the first 100 yards from the
trailhead along the right side of the river and then goes left into the forest.
For three miles this well-worn trail parallels the Fryingpan River,
sometimes through small clearings, but mostly through the woods. After
passing through a beautiful pine forest, the trail roller-coasters through an
area with very large boulders.

After the three miles you will come to an intersection of trails and a sign.
Take a right up through the trees on the Granite Lakes Trail, climbing at
first gradually, then quite steeply up a series of switchbacks. You will pass a
lookout point and continue to climb steeply through the woods to the right
of the rushing and roaring Granite Creek. At 10,500 feet elevation you will
come to a very picturesque stream crossing in the woods. On the other side
of the stream stay right on the muddy trail as it splits and closely parallels

Upper Granite Lake.

the stream. In about 20 minutes you will cross a small side stream and come out onto a very flat meadow known as Rangers' Meadow, because the rangers camped here while working on the trail. The trail exits the meadow at the far end on the right, crosses the creek, and begins to head up the right side of the stream valley, crossing a number of heavily bouldered areas. You will continue to climb steeply over rocky terrain.

About 40 minutes from Rangers' Meadow you will come to the top of a flatter area strewn with boulders and scattered trees below a slight ridge. From here you will have just one more section of slightly steeper climbing before reaching the trees in a fairly level area before the lake. Stay on the main trail, cross the small outlet stream, and you'll be at the lake. The elevation of this lower lake is 11,380 feet.

To get to the second lake, find the main trail which exits from the left side of the lake. The trail will gradually ascend, continuing on the same heading you used to approach the lower lake. After crossing a rocky area, the trail climbs up the side of a slope and into a few trees. As you pass through a marshy and wet area with water coming down from above, the trail disappears. Beware of mistaking elk trails for the main trail. Cross the wet area and stay straight ahead to climb uphill over the ridge ahead of you. You will have to do some bushwhacking and should watch the map closely. This route takes you up onto the ridge a little above the second lake from where you bear right and drop down to the lake. Stay left at the lake, cross the outlet stream, and look for a camping site in the trees by the lake.

Redstone/Marble

The two small towns of Redstone and Marble are located in the beautiful Crystal River Valley. The Crystal River, which originates at Schofield Pass, is fed by melting snow and crystal clear springs, hence its name. The river passes through some of the most spectacular scenery in the Rockies as it flows by the ghost towns of Schofield and Crystal City on its way to Marble and Redstone.

Redstone, a quaint town that houses Victorian cottages, the Redstone Castle, and the Redstone Inn, is the western gateway to the Maroon Bells-Snowmass Wilderness. There are fewer trails and less crowds in the Redstone end of the wilderness area than in the Aspen end, but many consider the Redstone side to be more attractive. The Avalanche Creek Trail and the East Creek Trail are the two major entry trails.

Route #33 lays out a day hike up the Avalanche Creek Trail, while Route #34 describes a spectacular multiday loop using both the Avalanche Creek Trail and the East Creek Trail, with optional alternative routes to vary the length of the trip. The region around Avalanche and Capitol lakes, accessed by the Avalanche Creek Trail, is one of my favorite backcountry areas. The East Creek Trail, one of the steepest and least used trails in the wilderness, is an ideal route for someone seeking a challenge, adventure, and isolation.

The town of Marble is best known as the site of the Yule Marble Quarry where the marble for the Tomb of the Unknown Soldier and many other monuments and buildings was quarried. The white marble up Yule Creek was first discovered in the 1870s. In the 1890s the quarrying of marble started a boom that replaced mining. After several periods of inactivity, the Yule Marble Quarry is still in operation today. An interesting side trip from Marble, for those with a four-wheel drive vehicle, is the six- mile drive from Marble to Crystal City and the historic Crystal Mill, one of the most photographed structures in all of Colorado.

Marble is bounded by two wilderness areas—the Raggeds Wilderness to the south and the Maroon Bells-Snowmass Wilderness to the north. Route #35 takes the hiker up the Raspberry Creek Valley to Marble Peak in the Raggeds Wilderness and offers a couple of alternate routes for the return trip, one being a side trip to the Yule Marble Quarry (which may be closed to the public—check before starting the hike). Route #36 goes into the Maroon Bells-Snowmass Wilderness from the south, and can be done as a long day hike or an overnight camping trip. This loop goes through a wide variety of terrain highlighted by an abundance of wildflowers in the summer and the beautiful golden hues of the aspen in the fall.

33. Avalanche Creek Trail

Start/Destination: Avalanche Campground/Duley Park
(7,310/8,480 feet)
Round-trip Distance/Hiking Time: 5–11 miles/4–8 hours
Elevation Range: 7,310–8,480 feet
Maps: p. 82–83; USGS Redstone; TI #128
Wilderness Designation: Maroon Bells-Snowmass Wilderness

General Comments: The trip along Avalanche Creek, described as a
day hike here, can be extended into a multiday backpacking trip (see Route
#34). The trail follows Avalanche Creek up the beautiful, rocky-walled
Avalanche Creek Valley. I would suggest going at least as far as Hell
Roaring Creek, but try to make it to Duley Park. The mostly wooded
Avalanche Creek Trail is very easy to follow and climbs gently up the
valley, making this an extremely pleasant day hike.

Directions to Trailhead: From Highway 82 in Carbondale (12 miles
southeast of Glenwood Springs, 29 miles northwest of Aspen) turn south
onto Highway 133. Drive 12.2 miles to Road 310 on the left with a sign for
Avalanche Creek. Cross the bridge over the Crystal River and follow this
gravel road 2.5 miles to Avalanche Campground and the parking lot at the
end of the campground. The trail leads out of the end of the parking lot; the
trail register is 100 feet down the trail.

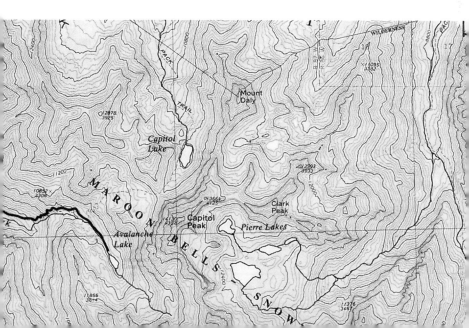

Trail Route: Follow the well-worn trail from the parking lot as it parallels Avalanche Creek on the left. In about one-third mile you will pass the wilderness boundary sign and continue on a very gentle ascent. As the trail starts ascending up away from the creek, it enters beautiful stands of tall aspen and brings you through a wooded area, separated from the main valley by a knoll. When you come to the top of the ascent (you are now about 2½ miles from the start of the hike), you will pass a small path and a sign on the left for the Hell Roaring Trail #1960. Keep going straight and in a couple of minutes, after a switchbacking descent, you will cross a bridge over the gorgeous, cascading Hell Roaring Creek in a rocky gorge.

The trail continues on a long descent to the cascading Avalanche Creek on the narrow valley floor. From this point you will be passing through a variety of terrain close to the creek with views of the rocky peaks ahead. A little over 2½ miles from the Hell Roaring Trail intersection you will encounter a sloping open area, and in another one-quarter mile will reach a large, grassy meadow. This meadow, surrounded by aspen and conifer, and highlighted by a stand of straight aspen at the far end, is Duley Park

34. Avalanche/East Creek Loop

Start/Destination: Avalanche Campground/Redstone (7,310/7,150 feet)
Round-trip Distance/Hiking Time: 17–25 miles/3–5 days
Elevation Range: 7,150–12,120 feet
Maps: p. 82–83; USGS Redstone, Capitol Peak; TI #128
Wilderness Designation: Maroon Bells-Snowmass Wilderness

General Comments: This backpacker's loop passes through some of the most beautiful backcountry in the Maroon Bells-Snowmass Wilderness. As described here, the route goes from Avalanche Campground to Avalanche Lake, back to the East Creek Trail, and up this trail over a high ridge into Redstone (about a 25-mile trip). Good camping sites abound along the entire route; since the trails follow streams, water is plentiful. The loop can be shortened to 17 miles by omitting Avalanche Lake, or the East Creek Trail can be omitted, making this an out-and-back trip to Avalanche Lake of 22 miles. Only experienced hikers should attempt the East Creek Trail portion of the route. This section is very steep, and at the higher elevations the trail is difficult to follow.

Some of the variations off this route: a side trip can be made to Capitol Lake; the Silver Creek Trail can be taken towards Crystal and Marble; the Hell Roaring Trail can be taken to the Capitol Creek Trail for a big loop (see *Aspen-Snowmass Trails*, Route #30).

Passing through an open area on the Avalanche Creek Trail.

Since the route described here begins at Avalanche Campground and ends in Redstone, you will either have to drop a car in Redstone or have someone pick you up there at the end of the hike. You can also try to catch a ride from Redstone back to the trailhead, not always an easy task.

Directions to Trailhead: Same as Route #33.

Trail Route: Follow the route as described in Route #33 to Duley Park. The trail leaves Duley Park through a stand of beautiful, straight aspen. Almost a mile past the park you will pass through the right edge of a clearing and then in less than one-half mile will come to a junction with the signed East Creek Trail going off to the right. If you're not going to Avalanche Lake, take the right here to continue up along Gift Creek on the East Creek Trail towards Redstone. Otherwise, remember this junction for your return trip and continue straight toward Avalanche Lake.

After the junction the trail to Avalanche Lake climbs and gets rockier. Across the valley to the right the dramatic Gift Creek drainage is visible. About three miles from the East Creek Trail junction, the trail starts switchbacking up the valley wall until it reaches Avalanche Creek cascading down very steeply through a beautiful rock canyon. After crossing a side stream and steadily climbing through the woods, the trail levels somewhat as you come to the intersection with the Capitol Creek Trail going up to the left. Stay straight, and in 10 minutes you will come to a sign in a clearing for the Silver Creek Trail on the right. From here it's only 10–15 minutes to Avalanche Lake. The lake is encircled by rock, basins, ridges—a gorgeous setting. You may want to camp in the trees next to the lake, but camp at least 100 feet from the water. If you have the time, spend an extra day to take some exploratory hikes up beyond the lake.

To continue on the multiday loop, go back down the trail from Avalanche Lake to the East Creek Trail (about 4 miles). Follow the trail to the left to Avalanche Creek. Cross Avalanche Creek, then walk up along the left side of Gift Creek to find a place to cross over to the right side, where you will pick up a faint trail heading up through the rocks alongside the creek. The trail leaves the rock slide, enters the woods, and climbs along the waterfall-filled creek very steeply through old-growth forest.

A little over a mile up, the trail starts heading away from the creek to the right through an open area and enters another drainage. This is an excellent area for camping. Keep following the main trail (avoid the fainter side trails) which heads straight up through the woods to the right of this new drainage. The trail will lead to two sinkholes in a sloped open area; from here head straight up along a slight ridge through the steep meadows above. At this point the trail is hard to follow and game trails are abundant, but perseverance will win out. The trail takes big switchbacks through the meadows and mostly stays to the right of the stream coming down from above, ending up in the basin on the right side of the stream. If you look up onto the ridge above, you may be able to see a wooden pole on the ridge—this is your goal.

As you come to a stream crossing, keep the rocky face on your right and then recross the stream to follow a long steep traverse to the right on a well-worn trail. This traverse and a few switchbacks will lead you to a saddle on the ridge at 11,220 feet where a post is stuck in some rocks. Continue up the ridge to the left and enjoy the spectacular views, especially behind you. Ignore the many side trails (game trails) as you head up along the top of the ridge. In about a mile you will reach another ridge which marks the top of your climb. On the other side is the East Creek drainage leading into the Crystal River Valley.

The trail, marked by a few cairns, drops down through the tundra and is hard to see in the upper part of the basin. Head down toward the right side of East Creek and pick up the trail which follows the creek. If you are ready to camp, the best place is at treeline—farther on the terrain will be a little too steep. After a couple more stream crossings, the trail follows the stream on the right and descends through a few open areas before steeply switchbacking down through the trees. The trail is very well worn and follows the creek, first through old conifer forest, then through aspen.

At about 8,850 feet the trail crosses to the left side of the creek, and after about two-thirds of a mile comes to the intersection with the Lily Lake Trail which goes left and is marked by a sign. Continue down to the right; in 15–20 minutes you will come to a stream crossing on a foot bridge, and then soon to a trail register and a gravel road. Follow the road to the right as it descends via long switchbacks for about ¾ mile to the paved road going through Redstone. From here it's about 8 miles back to the trailhead at Avalanche Campground. Take Highway 133 north to the Avalanche Creek turnoff and go right 2.5 miles to the campground.

35. Marble Peak Via Raspberry Creek Loop

Start/Destination: Marble/Marble Peak (7,920/11,314 feet)
Round-trip Distance/Hiking Time: 9 miles/6–8 hours
Elevation Range: 7,920–11,314 feet
Maps: p. 88; USGS Marble; TI #128
Wilderness Designation: Raggeds Wilderness

General Comments: This excursion into the Raggeds Wilderness from the Crystal River Valley takes you up the lovely Raspberry Creek Valley to Marble Peak, located on a ridge separating the White River National Forest from the Gunnison National Forest. From this vantage point you have a good perspective of the many peaks, valleys, and basins of the Maroon Bells-Snowmass Wilderness and the Raggeds Wilderness.

If you wish to make this a two-day trip, the best places to camp are in the upper Raspberry Creek Valley just below the ridge. One of the two options for a return-trip route from Marble Peak includes a side trip to the Yule Marble Quarry (sometimes closed to the public). Bring a map along on this hike and pay close attention to the trail description, especially for the upper portion of the hike near the ridge. In several places the trail is indistinct and game trails can cause some confusion.

Directions to Trailhead: From Highway 82 in Carbondale (12 miles southeast of Glenwood Springs, 29 miles northwest of Aspen) turn south onto Highway 133. Drive 22.5 miles to the Marble turnoff on the left (County Road 3). Follow this road, some of which is gravel, 6.1 miles to Marble to the road on the right next to the Volunteer Fire Department. Turn right onto this road (marked as the Yule Quarry Road) to the parking lot before the bridge, the start of your hike. Do not try to park on the Yule Quarry Road. The trailhead parking lot is right next to the remains of the Colorado Yule Marble Mill, a historic site which is worth a few extra minutes of your time to visit.

Trail Route: Cross the bridge by the parking lot and walk up the Yule Quarry Road. About one-quarter mile up the road is a trail going to the right with a sign for Raspberry Creek Trail #1969. Follow the trail as it winds up the face of the mountain. At a little over a mile, after ascending a small ridge with a gully off to the right, you will come to a trail junction with a sign indicating Anthracite Pass to the left and Raspberry Creek to the right. Stay right, following the narrow trail that contours around the front side of the mountain. You will see the town of Marble below, Beaver Lake and the Lead King Basin Road down to the right, and the towering Mount Daly across the valley. (Route #36 takes you around Mount Daly.)

In three-quarters of a mile the trail heads up to the left into the Raspberry Creek drainage. At a fork with a lower trail stay left through the aspen toward Raspberry Creek. Once you break into the open, you will be hiking through meadows full of wildflowers and raspberries. From the creek the trail takes you on a gradual uphill climb. When the trail fades in the high grass, watch for a few rock cairns as the trail switchbacks almost straight uphill and then continues its steady climb on a contour up the side of the mountain. Once in the trees you should expect to see wildlife—especially deer, elk, and grouse. In the tall spruce where the trail climbs more steeply, stay on the main well-worn trail, as many game trails head off to the side.

As the trail starts to contour to the right below the ridge, follow it only a short distance until you approach a high mound (marked 11,345 feet on the map). Cut up through the grassy basin before the rocky face to the low point on the ridge above. You will not see a distinct trail until you are on top of the ridge. Go left along the broad, flat, grassy ridge. Pick up the trail as it contours along the right side of the ridge, taking you a little below the first summit (from where a secondary ridge goes to the left) and bringing you out on top again for the short walk to the summit of Marble Peak.

The north side of the peak is a steep, rocky drop-off, while the south side is a sloped, grassy area bordered by a few trees. To the north you can see Capitol Peak, Snowmass Mountain, and other peaks of the Elk Mountain Range in the distance. Treasure Mountain (right) and Whitehouse Mountain (left) jut up across the Yule Creek Valley to the east.

After a lunch break on the peak, continue along the ridge for a couple of hundred yards to where the trail drops down off the ridge to the left. From here take the long dropping switchbacks through a sloped open area, until you've reached a group of tall conifers. Stay right of the trees and follow the trail as it angles down through the open area, cuts through a couple of gullies, goes above some spruce trees, and, after a steep section, eases off, descending a broad ridge into a flat grassy area with scattered trees. This flat grassy area, marked by a signpost on the left side, is Anthracite Pass.

From here you have two choices for your route back down to the trailhead. Alternative #1 is the most direct route, taking you down the old pack trail to the first part of the Raspberry Creek Trail. Alternative #2 takes you to the Yule Quarry Road, from where you can make a side trip to the quarry.

(Alternative #1) Looking towards Marble, take the trail on the left that starts off fairly level in the trees. The trail will cross a small drainage, another little gully, and then descend steeply through a conifer forest. Just under a mile from the pass the trail enters Mud Gulch, a drainage with steep, layered, rock walls above. After passing through meadows of wildflowers, about one-half mile from the gulch the trail crosses a small stream, continues through patches of raspberries and scattered aspen, and then winds down more steeply through the woods to the Raspberry Creek Trail which you take to the right, back down to the parking lot.

(Alternative #2) Looking towards Marble, take the trail on the right going down through the trees. The well-worn path switchbacks down through the tall conifers and comes to a small stream in a gully after about one-third mile. Follow the main trail down the left side of the stream (a pleasant shaded downhill) to a stream crossing and continue down the other side to the intersection with the Yule Pass Trail. Take the Yule Pass Trail down to the left, and in 2–3 minutes you will break into the open with the Yule Quarry Road visible ahead.

After 5 minutes of steep descent you will be at a trail register by the road. You have two choices:(a) Follow this gravel road down to the left for 3 miles to get back to the trailhead; you may be able to catch a ride down. (b) Go right to the Yule Marble Quarry. Be aware that the quarry is private property, and is sometimes closed to the public. Ten minutes up the road is the quarry parking lot from where a foot trail climbs along the cascading Yule Creek for about one-half mile to the quarry. The walk is steep, but pleasant, through the cool woods alongside piles of marble. To return, follow the Yule Quarry Road from the quarry parking lot down for about 3½ miles to the trailhead in Marble.

36. Carbonate Creek/Buckskin Basin Loop

Start/Destination: Carbonate Creek Trailhead (7,950 feet)
Round-trip Distance/Hiking Time: 12 miles/10 hours or 2 days
Elevation Range: 7,950–12,100 feet
Maps: p. 88; USGS Marble; TI #128
Wilderness Designation: Maroon Bells-Snowmass Wilderness

General Comments: This scenic route goes up Carbonate Creek, circles around Mount Daly, passes 12,100-foot Avalanche Pass, and drops down through Buckskin Basin. About half of the route is above timberline in the tundra, providing spectacular views and meadows ablaze with wildflowers. The many stands of aspen make this a good candidate for a colorful autumn hike. Much of the hike is very steep—the hike climbs over 4,000 feet in elevation to Avalanche Pass. Only well-conditioned and experienced hikers should try to do this route in a day.

Buckskin Basin is one of the most picturesque areas in the entire Crystal River Valley and would be the best place for backpackers to camp. At times the trail is somewhat difficult to follow, so map-reading skills and a good sense of direction are important. The last three miles of the loop are on a gravel road, so time can be saved by dropping a car at the North Lost Trail Trailhead, or by catching a ride at the end of the hike.

Directions to Trailhead: From Highway 82 in Carbondale (12 miles southeast of Glenwood Springs, 29 miles northwest of Aspen) turn south onto Highway 133. Drive 22.5 miles to the Marble turnoff on the left (County Road 3). Follow this road into Marble where you stay on the main road through town (take two sets of left & right turns, go over a bridge, take a left turn) to the Beaver Lake Lodge, 6.5 miles from Highway 133. The trailhead and parking space is behind the lodge.

Trail Route: From the Beaver Lake Lodge follow a path up through the weeds to the official trail register. The first section of trail passes through private property and is marked by small brown posts with arrows. The trail switchbacks up the mountainside, crosses a couple of roads, and continues in the aspen above a series of small waterfalls in Carbonate Creek. After the last road crossing you will descend to a stream crossing. Directly across the stream the trail goes sharply up to the right, then ascends steeply between two small drainages and through an aspen forest until it reaches an open area at 9,800 feet (about 2 miles from the trailhead).

The wildflower-filled meadows ahead of you will cause some route-finding problems. Horse and elk trails help confuse the issue and the main trail fades to obscurity. Follow the first trail that heads into the meadow and keep ascending. If you lose the trail, follow the meadow as far as you can up into a corner by some aspen trees. Pick up the trail in the trees; as you exit the trees the trail drops slightly, then continues on a contouring traverse up the steep valley wall. Ahead you will see the Carbonate Creek basin with the trail on the left. The trail heads past several waterfalls and across sloping meadows filled with wildflowers. Farther on, you will cross the stream and continue through small basins of rocks and wildflowers. Keep looking ahead for the trail as it fades in the tundra.

About a mile from the stream crossing the trail comes to the saddle above Buckskin Basin and a trail going up to the left to Avalanche Pass. It will take you about 10 minutes to get to the pass which overlooks a world of rocky peaks and a large valley in the Maroon Bells-Snowmass Wilderness. Retrace your steps from Avalanche Pass to the Buckskin Basin saddle and follow the trail as it descends into a basin of wildflowers, rockslides, tundra, and treed rocky knolls with a lovely stream.

As you get a little over a mile down from the saddle, sharpen up your trail-finding skills— the route can be confusing. At about 10,800 feet you will cross the stream and follow a series of switchbacks down to the left of the stream with the trees off to your left. Below a steep section of stream bed you will come to a second stream crossing which will take you to some long, gradual, traversing switchbacks on the other side. As the terrain starts to level off at 10,350 feet, you will come to a trail (North Fork Lost Trail Creek Trail); stay left on the trail into the woods. After 200 feet in the woods at a trail junction, take the trail (North Lost Trail) to the right as it winds down steeply onto a small ridge with streams and waterfalls on both sides. You will soon cross the creek on the left and follow the trail above the creek downhill through a beautiful forest of tall fir and aspen.

Ten minutes after another stream crossing you will reach the road (Lead King Basin Road) at a small parking area with trailhead signs. Walk down the road to the right, past the Colorado Outward Bound School. At the intersection of the Crystal River Jeep Trail, which goes to Lizard Lake and Crystal City, stay right and continue to the trailhead in Marble.

One of the lovely stands of aspen in the Crystal River Valley.

Index

N

Nast Lake Trailhead, 79
Native Lake, 9, 55, 58-59
New York Collection Canal, 49
New York Creek Trailhead, 49
Norrie, 73, 79
North Fork Lake Creek, 52
North Fork Lake Creek Trailhead, 52
North Fork Lost Trail Creek Trail,
    91-92
North Lost Trail, 92
North Lost Trail Trailhead, 90
North Mount Elbert Trail, 9, 61, 64

O

Old Snowmass, 9, 22, 31
Owl Creek, 21

P

Parry Peak Campground, 60
Pearl Pass Road, 37
Petroleum Lake, 9, 48-50
Petroleum Lake Trailhead, 48
Portal Campground, 48
Prince Creek Road, 34
Pyramid Peak, 13, 15, 29

R

Raggeds Wilderness, 7, 81, 87
Rangers' Meadow, 80
Raspberry Creek, 87-88
Raspberry Creek Trail, 9, 88-89
Raspberry Creek Valley, 81, 87
Red Mountain, 22, 25
Redstone, 9-10, 81, 84-85, 87
Redstone Castle, 81
Redstone Inn, 81
Rio Grande Trail, 25, 27

Road 105, 57, 59, 75
Road 300, 57, 59, 64
Road 310, 83
Road 311, 34
Road 501, 68-70
Road 504, 73
Road 505, 77
Roaring Fork River, 23, 47
Roaring Fork Valley, 11, 23, 34-36
Ruby, 50
Ruedi Reservoir, 5, 67

S

San Isabel National Forest, 5
Savage Lakes, 68-69
Savage Lakes Trail, 9, 69
Savage Lakes Trailhead, 69
Savage Peak, 70-71
Sawatch Range, 70
Sawmill Park, 29
Sawyer Lake, 68, 73
Sawyer Lake Trail, 9, 73
Scenic Trail, 15, 17
Schofield, 39, 81
Schofield Pass, 39, 81
Schofield Pass Road, 9, 18, 37, 39, 42,
    44
Sellar Lake, 75
Shadyside Trail, 25
Silver Creek Trail, 84, 86
Silver Dollar Pond, 43
Snowmass Creek Road, 22
Snowmass Lake, 15-16
Snowmass Mountain, 15, 29, 89
Snowmass Ski Area, 22
Snowmass Village, 9, 11, 19, 22, 27
Sopris, Captain Richard, 35
Sopris Creek Road, 34
South Mount Elbert Trail, 10, 61-64
Spruce Creek, 27-28, 30
Spruce Creek Trail, 10, 27-30

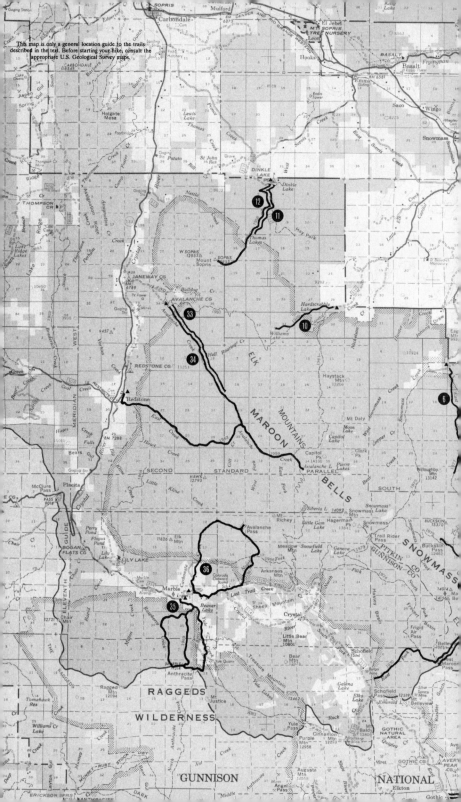